Midrashic Comments on the Torah

For Sabbaths and Festivals

by
Rabbi Abraham P. Bloch

Midrashic Comments on the Torah

For Sabbaths and Festivals

by
Rabbi Abraham P. Bloch

KTAV PUBLISHING HOUSE, INC.
HOBOKEN, NJ
1991

Copyright (c) 1991
Abraham P. Bloch
Library of Congress Cataloging-in-Publication Data

Bloch, Abraham P.
   Midrashic comments on the Torah : for Sabbaths and Festivals / by
Abraham P. Bloch
      p.   cm.
   ISBN 0-88125-377-4 : $19.95
   1. Jewish sermons, American.   2. Bible.   O.T.   Pentateuch-
-Sermons.   3. Festival-day sermons. Jewish.   I. Title.
BM740. 2.B47   1991
296.1'4--dc20   91-25735
                                                                CIP

Manufactured in the United States of America

*This book is lovingly dedicated
to our great grandchildren*

Chaim Yitzchok, Avi, Shirah, and Arielle

Rochel and Yoni

Abigail and Yisroel Meir

Contents

Contents

Introduction

RESISTANCE TO THE encroachments of paganism and the pursuit of social justice were the primary goals of the Hebrew prophets. The end of the threat of a relapse to heathenism ushered in the era of Rabbinic Judaism.

The rabbinic leadership continued the ongoing pursuit of social justice, but its main mission was the exposition of biblical law and the composition of a legal code to meet the needs of a developing Jewish society. To that end it created two new institutions, the academy and the synagogue.

The development of jurisprudence was exclusively in the domain of the academy. Exegetical discourses were delivered at the bet hamidrash, which was filled with laymen on Friday evenings and Saturday afternoons. Out of the bet hamidrash issued the lectures which made up the Midrash.

The legal and midrashic dissertations were all components of the Oral Law. Both were committed to memory, and brevity was indispensable to the process. Unfortunately, excessive brevity occasionally blurs the meaning of a statement. Brief mishnaic dicta were regularly elaborated in the Gemara. Midrashic passages, however, retained an enigmatic style, waiting for eventual clarification.

Mishnah and Gemara address the mind, Midrash addresses the heart. The intent of midrashic exegesis was not the elucidation of obscure biblical terms but the extraction of ethical principles and the transmission of encouraging sentiments to bolster the flagging spirits of the people.

The early church was keenly aware of the influence of the Midrash on the Jewish masses. On February 13, 553, Emperor Justinian of the Byzantine Empire ordered the reading of a Greek translation of the weekly portion of the Torah in all synagogues on Shabbat

1

mornings. He also prohibited the delivery of midrashic interpretations of the Torah.

The Midrash is still a valuable source of inspiration and guidance. It is my hope that the midrashic interpretations in this book will contribute to a better understanding of some of the enigmatic midrashic passages quoted in its pages. My sincere thanks to Els Bendheim for her careful reading of the proofs and her many insightful suggestions.

Abraham P. Bloch

BERESHIT

Preserving the Environment

The world was created by ten utterances [Vayomer], i.e. Vayomer is mentioned ten times in the biblical text. [The world] could have been created by a single utterance [on the first day] but [God desired] to mete out a harsher punishment [as a deterrent] to the wicked who destroy a world created by ten utterances and to increase the reward of the righteous who preserve a world created by ten utterances.

Abot 5; Yalkut Shimoni, Bereshit 1

WHEN THE CREATION of the world was completed, God placed Adam in the Garden of Eden and commanded him "to cultivate and preserve it" (Gen. 2:15). Even the lush land of the Garden of Eden was not immune to erosion. Oddly, the command to preserve the earth's natural resources predated by more than two thousand years the command to preserve one's life and health (Deut. 4:9).

Cain, the world's first full-time farmer, was guilty of violating some of the divine utterances. Like all primitive farmers, he failed to take proper measures to preserve the fertility and productiveness of the soil. The abundance of available land eliminated the need for conservation. The first step toward the destruction of a vital resource was taken by man. Indeed, the process of destruction began soon after the completion of the creation.

Cain's offering was rejected by God as a warning that contributions from illegal wealth are not acceptable. His violation of the fifth utterance (Gen. 1:11) might have appeared insignificant to him but it led to the violation of the ninth utterance (Gen. 1:26), when he committed murder.

The punishment of Cain was designed to fit his crime. He had destroyed the fertility of the land and now he was given a taste of his own negligence. He was told that whatever land he chose to till would fail to be productive. Driven endlessly in search of new land, he spent the rest of his life wandering over the face of the earth. Thus did he pay for the crime of murder.

Cainism is very much alive in the modern world. The harm done to the environment of the world by the continuing destruction of the Brazilian rain forest has been widely publicized. Industrial toxic wastes, recklessly scattered in many areas, poison land, water, and life in violation of the fourth (land and water), fifth (the produce of the earth), seventh (fowl and fish), eighth (animals and beasts) and ninth (man) utterances. The fate of Cain has not deterred the ravagers of our earth.

Adam was created by a single utterance. However, it takes hundreds of parental utterances to raise a child to adulthood. It takes thousands of utterances to raise a young Jew capable of transmitting our tradition to the next generation. We are unfortunately wasting our most important resource due to negligence and indifference of the Jewish community.

Jewish Roller-Coaster Existence

NOAH

Rabbi Samuel said: "There were five [men who beheld a new world]: Noah . . . Joseph . . . Moses . . . Job. . . . [and] Mordecai."

Bereshit Rabbah 30

THE EMERGENCE OF new worlds is not predictable because they do not evolve from older ones in the course of a normal evolutionary process. The new worlds which brought relief to the five men on Rabbi Samuel's list came as a surprise to most of them. Whenever Jews are plunged into the depth of an abyss, they look for some unexpected harbinger of salvation to keep despair from smashing their hopes and faith.

Rabbi Akiva saw the hand of God in Jewry's roller-coaster existence. Defeat and victory are divinely ordained and closely linked. The fulfillment of God's punishment argues for a similar fulfillment of God's promised rewards (Makkot 24b). Each catastrophe becomes a breeder of new hope.

The unpredictability of the time of the emergence of a new world was deemed by Rabbi Samuel to be a positive factor. His encouraging message was: "Never give up hope, even when the outlook is most bleak. A new world may be just at hand."

Implied in his assertion is also the obverse message: "Never take good fortune for granted. A less favorable new world may make a surprise appearance." The predicaments of Rabbi Samuel's five men each terminated a previous happy state of affairs. Noah had been God's favorite, Joseph was a pampered son, Moses was a member of the royal household, Job's children were alive and well, the Jews of Persia were the king's guests at his banquet.

The duration of any new world is also as unpredictable as the time

7

of its emergence. Corruption infected the earth soon after the flood. Joseph's influence died together with him and as a result his family outlived its welcome in Egypt. Mordecai's rise to power saved Persian Jewry from extinction but had no lasting impact on the precarious existence of subsequent Jewish generations. Only the enduring heritage of Moses remains a testimony to his new world.

The annals of postbiblical Jewry are filled with new worlds which have emerged and vanished without changing the chronic course of Jewish history. It was given to modern Jewry to behold two new worlds of supreme importance. The establishment of the United States of America set a precedent of freedom and equality for the Jews of the diaspora. The creation of Israel restored Jewish national independence. Both worlds had unlikely sources.

It was Ferdinand of Spain, a foe of Jews, who sent Columbus on his voyage of exploration. It was the bestiality of Hitler that mobilized international backing for the creation of Israel.

Converts of All Ages Are Welcome

LECH LECHA

Why was he [Abraham] circumcised at age ninety-nine? To teach us that if one [a non-Jew] seeks conversion [at an old age], let him not say; "I am old, how can I convert?" Let him learn from Abraham, who was circumcized at ninety-nine.

Tanchuma, Lech Lecha 17

[He was circumcised at ninety-nine to teach a lesson:] Do not close the door [in the face of the elderly] who seek conversion.

Bereshit Rabbah 46

THE FIRST MIDRASH addresses itself to potential reservations by the elderly: "Is it proper to give up a faith which one has practiced most of his life?" The second Midrash addresses itself to potential reservations by the Jewish community: "Should we welcome a stranger who has lived in error most of his life?" Both reservations are emphatically rejected.

According to our tradition, non-Jews are bound by the seven Noahide laws. These pre-Sinaitic laws do not include the rite of circumcision, which was given exclusively to Abraham. The realization that this set him apart from all other nations led Abraham to express some fears that the noncircumcised might suspend their social intercourse with him (Bereshit Rabbah 46). Some nations might even attempt to stop the rite (Yalkut 17) and nip the new religion in the bud.

In modern times circumcision has been emptied of its religious significance. The adoption of circumcision by the general community on hygienic grounds has severed its link to the ancient covenant. Circumcision performed by a physician becomes a surgical procedure. The importance of circumcision as a religious rite must be reemphasized to Jews and converts alike.

The growth of the Jewish community through the addition of converts has become a factor in demographic assessments of the future of Jews and Judaism. Whatever objections were raised in the Talmud to the encouragement of conversions were based primarily on suspicions which cast doubts on the sincerity of would-be converts. Indeed, the Torah mentions the conversion of all of Abraham's servants. Yet none of them, according to rabbinic tradition, remained with the Jewish people (Pirke d'Rabbi Eliezer). Nevertheless, Jews traditionally welcome converts with open arms, as indicated in the two Midrashim above.

The midrashic explanation of Abraham's late circumcision conveys a broad message: The sinner, the bigot, the boor, the hypocrite, and all who wish to give up their undesirable life-style should bear in mind that any time is a good time for a change. One's age should never be a factor in a decision to break with the past.

Vanished Role Models

How many benedictions should be recited each day? Our masters taught: "One should recite eighteen." Why eighteen? Rabbi Samuel the son of Nachman said: "To match the eighteen Torah references to the three Patriarchs." [Each phrase refers to the three patriarchs. The first is in Gen. 50:24.] Rabbi Yochanan said: "To match the eighteen repetitions of the phrase 'As God had commanded Moses,' relating to the setting up of the Tabernacle." [The first phrase is in Exod. 38:22.]

Tanchuma, Vayera 1

THE PRAYER KNOWN as the "Eighteen" (*Shemoneh Esrei*) forms the core of the three daily prayer sessions. Its first three declaratory benedictions proclaim the majesty of God. The next three supplicatory benedictions plead that we may be enabled to comprehend the Torah and adhere to its commands, and that our sins be forgiven.

Jewish concern for the perpetuation of the faith takes precedence in our prayers over concerns for health, peace, and the restoration of Zion, themes of subsequent benedictions. Rabbi Samuel pointed to references highlighting the succession of three patriarchal generations. The success of each rested on his position as a role model. Hence his conclusion that a traditional home is the prime guarantor of the survivability of Judaism.

Rabbi Yochanan pointed to the eighteen phrases that highlight God's commands to Moses, the teacher and leader of the Jewish community. The responsibility for the viability of the Torah lies with the community and the educational facilities which it provides.

The "Eighteen" prayer begins with a salutation to "the God of Abraham, the God of Isaac, and the God of Jacob." Unlike Rabbi Samuel's interpretation, which stresses the role of the home, the

11

prayer reflects a doctrine of transference of merit, whereby offspring of a virtuous ancestor receive favorable consideration in heavenly judgment. There is no transfer of merit from teacher to student. For this reason we recall our descent from the Patriarchs rather than our discipleship of Moses.

While Rabbis Samuel and Yochanan differed as to the relative importance of home or school to the future of Judaism, they surely agreed that the joint efforts of both are vital to the continuity of the Torah heritage.

The rapid assimilation of modern Jews coupled with the growing instability of the Jewish family structure have undermined the effectiveness of the Jewish home as a factor in religious continuity. The deterioration of religious education has similarly undermined the effectiveness of the school as a factor in the perpetuation of Judaism. So long as Jewish education is not restored to the forefront of communal responsibility, the future of our Torah will continue to rest on two shaky legs.

Premature Aging

Rabbi Joshua bar Nachmani said: "Premature aging is triggered by four causes—fear, aggravation brought on by one's children, an evil wife, and war."

Tanchuma, Chaye Sarah 2

OLD AGE BEGINS, according to the rabbis, at sixty. One who reaches seventy (*seivah*) enters advanced age (Abot 5).

Impairment of physical functions and forgetfulness are endemic to old age (*ziknah*). Senility, characterized by disorientation and lack of comprehension, is quite common in some people of advanced age. When senility affects a person under sixty, he is deemed to have aged prematurely.

Judaism is unique in enjoining respect of old age: "Thou shalt rise before people of advanced age [*seivah*] and behave beautifully in the presence of an old man [*zaken*]" (Lev. 19:32; my trans.). We are bid to relate to an old person with correct behavior. When we rise in the presence of a person of advanced age, even if he is senile, we pay homage to one who has survived life's many pitfalls. At the same time we honor God, who has bestowed longevity upon him.

Following the burial of Sarah, Abraham is described in the Torah as being "old and advanced in days" (Gen. 24:1). The descriptive duplication is intended, according to the rabbis, to indicate that Abraham's old age was chronological ("advanced in days") and not premature.

Rabbi Joshua's list of four causes of premature aging is addressed to the incidence of senility. Insecurity induced by fears and war conditions creates a state of panic which leads to mental and emotional aberrations. Stressful aggravations produce intense anxieties which becloud the human mind. An "evil wife" is defined in

13

the Midrash as a young woman who is disrespectful of her aging husband. A great disparity in the ages of spouses was common in ancient times. The husband who is repeatedly subjected to indignities loses the self-respect essential for normal life. In the opinion of Rabbi Joshua, emotional strain is at the root of early senility.

Senior-citizen homes have programs to ease the problems of aging. The majority of the residents of these institutions are chronologically old but not senile. These citizens need to have their minds intellectually stimulated by lectures, discussions, study sessions, etc., to prevent mental stagnation.

Unfortunately, there is a common misconception that old age is identical with senility. Such misconceptions linger on and help shape the types of programs offered in most homes for the aged. Those who stress entertainment, to the total exclusion of intellectual stimulation, are inadvertently contributing to the development of senility.

Jacob, the Principal Patriarch

TOLDOT

When Nimrod cast Abraham into the furnace, the Holy One, blessed be He, came down to rescue him. The angels protested: "Master of the Universe, are You going to save Abraham? [Think of] the wicked persons [resha'im] who will issue from him" [Ishmael and Esau]. The Holy One, blessed be He, replied: "I will save him for the sake of Jacob."

Tanchuma, Toledot 4

ABRAHAM AND ISAAC SIRED one wicked son each, but there were wicked sons among the offspring of Jacob as well. To name but a few: King Ahab, the Hellenizer Jason, Pablo Christiani, Paul de Burgos, and Johannes Pfefferkorn. Surely no one will deny them the title of *rasha*. Why was Jacob free of guilt?

The angels, in the midrashic scenario, obviously did not hold Abraham accountable for the misdeeds of his wicked descendants. They were not referring to individuals named Ishmael and Esau. They were referring to religious movements and nations that claimed the two as their patriarchs and founders. Ishmael was the rabbinic code-name for neighboring Arab tribes, and Edom (Esau) was the code-name for the Roman Empire, pagan and Christian.

Shocked by the future bloody violence and hostility of these peoples and their religious movements toward the offspring of Abraham, the angels reflected that it would be preferable to surrender Abraham to Nimrod. This would prevent the birth of the two daughter-religions and their endemic hostility. God replied that Jacob was his choice and Abraham must be saved for his sake.

The rabbis were used to scenes of warring religions. Monotheism and polytheism naturally could not coexist. Yet the notion of a monotheistic offshoot religion that would adopt many of the theo-

15

logical doctrines, rituals, and ethical concepts of the mother religion, then turn against it and declare it obsolete and rejected by God, was most galling and shocking. How would the world react to the conduct of an invited guest who comes to the home of a host and is permitted to take some of its treasures only to turn on his host and attempt to burn down the house?

Nationalism, like religion, has filled the pages of human history with demonstrations of ingratitude. Medieval Jews were frequently its victims. Some states would invite Jews to come and enrich them with their financial skills and industriousness. No sooner had this goal been attained than the benefactors were expelled.

The post World War II Marshall Plan is another example. The impoverished nations which benefited most from American generosity became the foremost critics of American policies. As for individual ingratitude, it is a plague which is immune to religious censure and social condemnation.

The Slippery Top of Jacob's Ladder

VAYETZE

The Almighty let Jacob see the guardian angels [code word for the spirit of a nation] of Babylonia ascend and descend [The ladder], of Media ascend and descend, of Greece ascend and descend, and of Edom [Rome] ascend and descend. God then said to Jacob: "Jacob, why don't you go up?" Whereupon Jacob was seized with fear and said: "The others had to come down [from the top]. I, too, will end up at the bottom." The Almighty reassured him. "If you go up, you will not have to come down." Jacob did not believe it and he did not go up.

Tanchuma, Vayetze 2

THE ROUND TRIP of the angels began at the bottom because that is the starting point of all nations climbing the ladder of power. The ascent and descent of the nations listed in the Midrash illustrates the transience of military might. Babylonia, Persia, Greece, and Rome, nations which had all affected the course of Jewish history, each had its turn on the ladder. They reached the top and built empires only to crumble in the end as they toppled to the bottom.

God did not favor a powerful Jewish empire built at the expense of weaker nations. The borders of Eretz Yisrael were fixed in the Torah "from the Wadi-el-Arish to the Euphrates" (Gen. 15:18). The borders were subsequently redrawn "from Dan to Beer-Sheva" (II Sam. 17:11). Wars beyond the borders were sanctioned only in self-defense against hostile nations (Malbim, Sifri, Deut. 21:10). Preemptive wars in self-defense were not excluded. God promised Jacob that the strong nation which he would establish upon reaching the top of the ladder would endure for all time.

Jacob did not disbelieve God. However, he knew that God's promise

17

was conditional. So long as his offspring abided by the Torah and maintained a high ethical stature, the covenant would remain inviolable. Disobedience, however, would provoke divine retribution (Lev. 26:14–43). Jacob could not believe that his offspring would never be guilty of a breach of loyalty to God. To avoid an eventual free fall, he refused to climb the ladder.

According to another Midrash, the ladder did not symbolize the road to power but the effort to advance to higher moral values. "The ladder stood on the ground of Beer-Sheva [the home of Abraham] and its top reached the Temple" [the center of the Torah]" (Bereshit Rabbah 69). Indeed, Jacob climbed that ladder and reached the top, and his offspring have never left it.

Modern Israel has been portrayed by its enemies as expansionist. The accusation is groundless. Israel returned captured territory to Egypt for the sake of peace. Its military actions have always been shaped by the dictates of self-defense. It has never tarnished the moral standard of the top of the ladder.

An Unsafe House

May our master enlighten us: How many situations lead to the opening of a person's record [by the Heavenly Tribunal] for scrutiny [to determine whether he is deserving of God's special favor]. Our masters taught thus: "On three occasions is the file opened: when one travels on a road alone, when one lives in an unsafe house, and when one pledges [a contribution to charity] and does not pay."

Tanchuma, Vayishlach 8

"DINAH, THE DAUGHTER of Leah . . . went out to see the daughters of the land" (Gen. 34:1). Was Dinah's venture prompted by naivete or by a reckless disregard of risk, in the belief that God would keep her from harm? In accepting the latter assumption, the sages unequivocally condemned any disregard of reality. He who relies on a miraculous intervention is cautioned not to take lightly the prospect of being found wanting in the eyes of heaven.

Do the three situations in the Midrash have something in common? They do. Each one represents a life of pretense. The lone walker and the occupant of the unsafe home falsely pretend to possess great courage with the intent of gaining undeserved admiration. The bogus contributor flaunts a false generosity for the same reason.

If we read between the lines, we may discover another message which links the three individuals. The lone walker defiantly leaves the mainstream of public opinion to take action and pursue policies of his own. He mocks the common fears of the masses and sets out to disprove the presence of highway robbers who seek to harm innocent travelers. The robbers may indeed embrace him in order to lure the multitudes who will follow. Such was the case of the five

19

lone walkers who shook hands with Arafat to the outrage of the Jewish masses.

One who excludes Judaic influences from his home, claiming that a Jewish environment is not essential to the raising of Jewish children, lives in an unsafe house which poses a danger to the future of the Jewish people.

The definition of "Jewish home" is vague in the minds of many Jews. It cannot be measured by the ethnicity of the occupant. If objects symbolic of Jewish traditions and culture are not visible to the eye, and echoes of the sounds of Sinai do not reach the ears, the house is not Jewish.

If an individual assumes the mantle of Jewish leadership, pledging to pursue a course of action that will solve some of our critical problems, but in the end confines his activity to empty rhetoric, he is morally more debased than the person who fails to redeem his pledge. He betrays the trust of the people and besmirches the mantle of leadership.

History will take a close look at the record of these three types of individuals, and they may be found wanting in the eyes of God and the people.

Relative and Absolute Wrongs

VAYESHEV

"And Joseph was brought down to Egypt" [Gen. 39:1]. Do not read hurad [he was brought down], read horid [he brought down] his father and the tribes to Egypt.

Tanchuma, Vayeshev 4

GOD HAD REVEALED to Abraham that his offspring would experience a period of enslavement (Gen. 15:4). Its exact date was not indicated. Some rabbis felt that the appropriate time of its inception was soon after Joseph had been sold into slavery in Egypt. As the nominal suzerain of Canaan, Egypt could have forced Jacob and his family to "come down with chains around their necks." God, however, preferred a more dignified migration. So He arranged "Jacob's love of Joseph, the enmity of the brothers, the sale to the Ishmaelites, and the migration of Jacob at the invitation of Joseph" (Tanchuma, Vayeshev 4). The suggested alternative reading, *horid*, foreshadowed Joseph's initiative in the migration of the Hebrews to Egypt.

The Midrash incidentally exonerates Jacob from a charge of breach of ethical conduct. Parental favoritism is condemned in the Talmud (Shabbat 10b). It was not Jacob but God who willed this favoritism. Is the Midrash implying that God sanctions the use of wrongful means to attain a desirable goal?

There are several categories of wrongs. Some shed their wrongfulness under certain conditions. For instance, it is wrong to hit a child, but parents may use the rod as a disciplinary tool. To restrain an innocent individual is criminal, but it is proper to restrain a violent person. To lie is wrong, but a white lie, which benefits some and hurts none, is not considered a wrong.

Some actions are intrinsically wrong under all circumstances and

21

yet are frequently committed, in the expectation that some good will flow from them. This is the Robin Hood syndrome, which bestows a glow of heroism upon the perpetrator.

A third category consists of absolute wrongs which are not intended to be used as a means to a meritorious end.

Man, endowed with free will, is capable of initiating every kind of wrongful act. However, he is not capable of gauging the effects of his act nor of balancing the wrong against the right. He must therefore desist from such acts.

Blessings and curses may emanate from God, but we must never attribute absolute wrongs to Him. Whatever He does has a purpose and a reason, which we may not perceive or comprehend. This is the sense of the talmudic aphorism: "Whatever the All-Merciful does is for [the purpose of attaining] good" (Berachot 60b). God inspired Jacob to favor Joseph in order to spare him the fate of a captive transported in chains.

Hide Yourselves

And Jacob saw that food could be purchased in Egypt, and he said to his sons: "Why do you look one upon the other [Lamah Titra'u]?" [Gen. 42:1]. Jacob said to his sons: "Do not show in public that you are well fed, not in the presence of Esau and not in the presence of Ishmael, lest they envy you."

Taanit 10b

ACCORDING TO RABBINIC lore, Jacob asked his sons to join the many people who were going to Egypt to purchase food, even though he had enough food to tide him over for a while. It was a public relations problem rather than hunger which lent his request a sense of urgency.

The rabbis interpreted *titra'u* ("to see oneself") as if it had been written *tar'u* ("to show"). Jacob was apprehensive of the envy of the neighbors, which might easily turn into hate. The midrashic text specifically singles out Esau and Ishmael as people whose envy should not be aroused. Esau and Ishmael were code names for Rome and the Arab tribes in whose midst substantial Jewish minorities had settled.

Another Midrash expressed Jacob's anxieties more directly. "Jacob said to his children: 'I beg of you, hide yourselves from them, for nothing is as dangerous as an evil eye' " (Yalkut 42). The rabbis were obviously laying down a policy and guidelines for their contemporary and future generations in the guise of an interpretation of a biblical verse. "Hide yourselves," and do not attract the attention of a hostile government and the masses, was a preventive motto designed to safeguard the physical survival of the Jew.

Medieval Jewry, though isolated in a locked ghetto, did not escape regular contacts with the government and the people. Commerce

23

and banking brought the Jew face to face with the outside world. What is more, church had its theological reasons for stirring up hate of Jews and their religion, regardless of the lack of personal contacts.

The rabbinic policy of "Hide yourselves" shaped the decisions made by the ghettoized Jewry of the Middle Ages. Drastic steps were taken to avoid being thrust into the limelight or arousing the jealousy of non-Jews. Self-imposed sumptuary laws restricted lavish wedding affairs and prohibited the wearing of expensive garments.

The "Hide yourselves" motto has lost much of its rationale in modern democratic societies, where Jews contribute to the welfare of the state and enjoy full rights. The resurgence of interracial hatred is now combatted in the open rather than by hiding. Nevertheless echoes of the old policy still reverberate in our ears. Muted Jewish reactions during the Nazi era prove the influence of these echoes.

An Aggressive Approach

Joseph noticed Judah's rising anger. To avoid embarrassment in front of the Egyptians, he [suddenly] announced: "I am your brother Joseph."

Tanchuma, Vayigash 3

THE ABOVE MIDRASH explains why Judah's second plea was more effective than the previous pleas and denials of any criminal activity. One would be inclined to attribute the effectiveness of the second plea to its stirring eloquence as well as to its tugging at Joseph's conscience for contributing to the plight of his aged father. The only embarrassment Joseph feared was a possible display of emotional weakness in the presence of Egyptians. According to the Midrash, he feared being embarrassed by Judah's anger.

This simple explanation of the dramatic sequel of events was not accepted by some midrashic exegetists. Instead, they created a dialogue between Joseph and Judah in which Judah hurled accusations and threats. His new belligerence was the decisive factor leading to Joseph's self-identification. "When [Joseph] saw ten powerful men in front of him, each of whom could destroy ten lands, he became alarmed" (Tanchuma, Vayigash 4). "When Joseph saw that the brothers had decided to destroy Egypt, he said to himself, I had better identify myself before they destroy Egypt," (ibid. 5). Judah also accused Joseph of bigotry. "People came from many lands to Egypt to buy food, yet none of them was ever interrogated by you," (ibid.).

Rabbi Judah based the rabbinic assumption of a belligerent confrontation on the term *vayigash*, which opens this portion of the Torah. In II Samuel (10:13) the term conveys an "approach to do war." Other rabbis disagreed, quoting sources where *vayigash* in-

25

dicates an approach to arrange a conciliation, to conclude peace, to pray, etc. (Yalkut, Vayigash 44).

The abundant midrashic material favoring the interpretation that there was a confrontational encounter between Joseph and Judah apparently reflects a wish to formulate guidelines for future generations to shape their response to bigoted attacks. In the previous portion, Miketz, we discussed the rabbinic formulation of the "Hide thyself," stay out of the limelight, policy. If, however, Jews are attacked, despite their low profile, the rabbis suggested an activist counterattack policy. Bigots are not interested in the authenticity of their accusations, and are not impressed when they are proven false. Those who deny the Holocaust are not deterred by overwhelming evidence which confirms it. They can only be silenced by a demonstration of their twisted minds and bigoted background.

Henry Ford continued to distribute the *Protocols of the Elders of Zion* despite its being a forgery. Only fear of embarrassment in court, in front of the nation, stopped him.

Jacob's Sword and Bow

VAYECHI

"I have given Shechem to you [Joseph] above your brothers, which I took out of the hand of the Amorite with my sword and my bow" [Gen. 48:22]. . . . "My sword" is prayer and "my bow" is entreaty."

Baba Batra 123a

A LITERAL RENDITION of "my sword and my bow" obviously presents some incongruities. It implies a total reliance on military strength, contrary to the declarations of the psalmist: "A king is not saved by the size of an army, a warrior is not rescued by sheer might" (33:16) and "For I trust not in my bow, neither can my sword save me" (44:7). Secondly, Jacob asserts his ownership of Shechem based on its having fallen to his sword. Jewish claims to Eretz Yisrael rest on God's promise to the Patriarchs. The borders of the land are fixed in the Torah. A military occupation beyond the borders would not provide permanent legal rights of ownership. Lastly, it was not Jacob who captured Shechem, nor did he supply the weapons used by his sons.

The Aggadah assumes that Jacob was referring to spiritual weapons, the counterparts of swords and bows. Swords are used in close encounters, arrows are projected at distant targets. In similar fashion, prayers are directed to an omnipresent God while pleas are addressed to distant authorities who are in a position to help. Incidentally, the Hebrew terms "with my bow" and "my plea" are practically identical (*bekashti, bakashati*). Jacob prayed to God and most likely appealed to the neighbors to maintain the peace. His claim to Shechem was based on his successful intervention.

Jews have traditionally used both spiritual weapons in times of stress. The Kohanim are said to have remained at their posts in the Temple even as the flames set by the Romans cut off their retreat. At

27

the same time Rabban Yochanan b. Zakkai pleaded with the Roman authorities for permission to open an academy for the peaceful development of rabbinic Judaism. This pattern was followed throughout history. When oppression threatened medieval Jewish existence, the synagogues resounded with prayers while delegations pleaded at royal courts or to the Vatican.

The spiritual and physical swords are not self-exclusive. The use of defensive weapons is legitimate when pleas for peace go unheeded. It was King David who declared: "Blessed is the Lord, my Rock, who trains my hand for war and my fingers for battle" (Ps. 144:1). One is reminded of the popular wartime jingle: "Praise the Lord and pass the ammunition."

SHEMOT

Yocheved, an Activist

SHEMOT

"And the king of Egypt spoke to the Hebrew midwives" [Exod. 1:15]. Rav and Samuel disagreed. One said: "They were a woman and her daughter, Yocheved and Miriam." The other said: "They were a daughter in-law and her mother in-law, Yocheved and Elisheva [Aaron's wife]."

Sotah 11b; Shemot Rabbah 1

THE TWO MIDWIVES are identified in the Torah as Shifrah and Puah. Rav and Samuel assumed that these were not their real names. Both rabbis were of the opinion that Yocheved was one of the midwives, but they did not agree on the identity of the second midwife. Does their discussion convey a message, or were they engaging in idle speculation?

Moses is described in the Torah as the only human being "whom the Lord knew face to face" (Deut. 34:10). Why was Moses granted such a unique and exalted privilege? Most Bible students look to his character to discover the particular trait which made him worthy of becoming an intimate of God.

Rav and Samuel expanded this research by examining the record of the lives of Moses' parents. Which of them possessed the precious gene that was transmitted to their son? Did either of them lead so meritorious a life as to be blessed by God with an outstanding son as a reward? According to the Torah, God indeed rewarded the midwives. "He made them houses *batim*" (Exod. 1:21). *Batim* also means "families," i.e., distinguished offspring.

Amram, the father of Moses, was, according to ancient Jewish lore, a highly prominent person. He was the head of the Sanhedrin (Shemot Rabbah 1), free of sin (Shabbat 55b), and the greatest man of his generation (Sotah 12a). However, he was not an activist who

31

took steps to frustrate Pharaoh's genocidal policies. He resigned himself to the doom of the Jewish people and advocated the cessation of any further procreation. The image of the man, as depicted in the ancient lore, is in total contrast to that of Moses, who began his involvement with the fate of his brethren in a burst of active opposition.

If Yocheved was one of the midwives, as the rabbis assumed, she appears in the role of a fighting activist who covertly succeeded in frustrating Pharaoh's hostile designs by saving the male infants. She was also said to have raised funds and collected food so that impoverished mothers could sustain the lives of their children (Shemot Rabbah 1). Moses was her divine reward.

Pinechas was another activist who saved the Jewish people from destruction (Num. 25:11). Assuming that Elisheva was the second midwife, her grandson Pinechas was her divine reward.

Scholars are traditionally the heroes of Jewish society. In times of danger, however, it is the rescuing activist who deserves the greatest honor.

Egyptian and Jew Drink from the Same Bowl

VA'EYRA

RABBI ABIN THE LEVITE SAID, "An Egyptian and an Israelite were in a home which had a tub of water. The Egyptian [who was thirsty due to the plague of blood] filled his jug, but the water turned into blood. Whereupon he said to the Israelite: 'Cup your hands and put some water into my mouth.' That also turned into blood. 'Let us drink together from a bowl,' the Egyptian continued. The Israelite drank water, but the Egyptian drank blood. Only when he paid a high price was the Egyptian able to drink water. Thus were the Hebrew slaves enriched."

Tanchuma, Va'eyra 13

THE EGYPTIAN NEEDED Jewish water to sustain his life. Water is the rabbinic symbol for the Torah (Baba Kama 17a). The early church needed the Jewish Bible to establish its legitimacy. Like the Egyptian, the church came to the Jewish home, Jerusalem, to appropriate parts of the Bible. Unlike the Egyptian, who was willing to let the Jew keep his share of the water, the church declared the Jewish part invalid and the Jew rejected by God. Alas, the water which the church drank turned into blood, the blood of Jewish martyrs who opposed the denigration of the Torah.

Frustrated by Jewish opposition, the church, like the Egyptian, hoped for greater success if the Jews were to hand over parts of their Torah. Jewish apostates cooperated, but the water which they brought along also turned into blood, Jewish blood.

The suggestion that Jews and Christians join in a fraternal setting to study and discuss the Bible was a more refined method which promised a quick fulfillment of a long-cherished dream—the conversion of the Jewish people. The Israelite had been willing to share his

33

water with the Egyptian because there was enough water to slake both thirsts. However, the Jews could not share their Torah with the Christians because the latter would not repudiate their missionary goal. Once again, whatever water the church obtained at such sessions turned into blood, bad blood. All of these successive stages appear to have been referred to in Rabbi Abin's allegorical fable of the Egyptian and the Israelite.

The payment of a high price is said to have been the only condition under which the Egyptian was able to obtain potable water. Indeed, the modern interfaith dialogue became feasible only when the church agreed to pay a high price. It had to concede that Judaism had not lost its validity and that God had not rejected the Jewish people. Furthermore, it also agreed, as did the Jews, that the dialogue, designed to promote better mutual understanding, was not to be tainted by covert missionary designs.

Let There Be Darkness

BO

"Stretch out thy hand toward heaven and let there be darkness"
[Exod. 10:21]. Whence did the darkness come? Rabbi Judah and
Rabbi Nehemiah [discussed it]. Rabbi Judah says: "From the
darkness on high. As it was said: 'He made darkness his hiding
place' " [Ps. 18:12]. Rabbi Nehemiah says: "From the darkness of
hell. As it is said: 'A land of thick darkness, as darkness itself'
[Job 10:22]."

Shemot Rabbah 14

THE GRAVITY OF EGYPT'S criminal behavior was reflected in God's ominous command, "Let there be darkness," a reversal of His initial command: "Let there be light." Egypt had morally degenerated into the primeval chaotic stage which had preceded the creation of light.

"Darkness" is commonly used as a figure of speech depicting either a lack of intellectual comprehension or a condition of emotional depression and pain. A scientist who seeks to comprehend a natural phenomenon but fails is said to be "in the dark." We also speak of people whose lives are "darkened" by many misfortunes.

What was the nature and intent of the darkness which enveloped Egypt? Rabbi Judah suggested that it was part of the darkness which surrounds God. Man is incapable of comprehending God and His ways. God appeared on Mount Sinai "in a thick cloud" (Exod. 19:9). Only Moses could "draw near unto the thick darkness." The psalmist's expression that "God made darkness His hiding place" is even more explicit.

The intent of the plague, according to Rabbi Judah, was educational rather than punitive. The darkness symbolized the intellectual failure of the Egyptians to perceive God's hand in their trying hour or the godliness in the anguished pleas of the Hebrews to be

35

freed from slavery. The plague of darkness offered the Egyptians an opportunity to ponder the meaning of their harsh experience and to mend their ways.

Rabbi Nehemiah disagreed. The Egyptians, he felt, were unable to respond to rational appeals and persuasion. Only force could make them change their minds. The darkness, according to him, came from hell.

The tragic chapter of American slavery supports Rabbi Nehemiah's view. Nothing short of death and destruction could bring about the abolition of slavery. The Nazi evil of our time was similarly unresponsive to appeals of reason. It had to be excised with a scalpel.

Rabbi Judah would probably have conceded that there are occasions when there is no alternative to force. However, he wanted to make sure that force is a tool of last resort.

Egyptian God-Fearers

B'SHALACH

"And he took six hundred chosen chariots" [Exod. 14:7]. Whose animals were hitched to the chariots? Did they belong to the Egyptians? No, for it was said, "And the cattle of Egypt died" [ibid. 9:6]. Did they belong to Pharaoh? No, for it was said: "The hand of the Lord is upon thy cattle which are in the field" [ibid. 9:3]. . . . Obviously they belonged to the God-fearers, who had saved their cattle by removing them from the field [ibid. 9:20]. It was the God-fearers' cattle which endangered Israel.

Tanchuma, B'Shalach 8

ONE MIGHT EXPECT the author of the Midrash to wonder how animals could have been available after a plague which had decimated them. However, he preferred to open his comment with an investigation of the identity of the owners of the animals which had been hitched to the chariots. This presented him with the opportunity to fulfill his main objective: to satirize the Egyptian God-fearers. They had feared God when the survival of their cattle was at stake but had defied God by giving their animals to Pharaoh when the survival of the Hebrews was at stake.

Medieval Jewry confronted a similar dilemma. The very people who professed a religion of love, compassion, and forgiveness treated Jews with hate, cruelty, and vindictiveness, all in the name of a loving and forgiving God.

Why did the Egyptian God-fearers disregard God's wish to free the Hebrew slaves from bondage? A religion based on fear alone is an ineffective educational and disciplinary force. Fear induces obedience to the dictates of one's faith but does not uplift one's character and ethical perceptions. The departure of the Hebrews put an end to the threat of new plagues. When the fear was gone, the "God-fearers" gave their full support to Pharaoh's oppressive rule.

Religion is similarly ineffective when based on love alone. People who express extreme love of God may be less than exemplary in their relations with their fellowman, on the theory that their love grants them a privileged position. Love of God framed by fear of God will keep an individual on a straight course.

The Hebrews, impressed by God's miracles in Egypt, "feared the Lord, and they believed in the Lord and in his servant Moses" (Exod. 14:31). Yet three days later they indicated at Marah their loss of faith in Moses (ibid. 15:24).

The emphasis on love and fear of God was implicit in two Deuteronomic injunctions. "Fear the Lord thy God" (6:2) is followed by "Love the Lord thy God" (6:5).

Those Who Hate Money

YITRO

"Sonei beza" [haters of unjust gain] [Exod. 18:21] refers to people who refuse to engage in litigation to collect outstanding debts. So says Rabbi Joshua. Rabbi Eleazar of Modiin says: "Sonei beza" are people who hate their own money [mamon azmom] and surely hate other people's money."

Mechilta, Exod. 18:21

THE NOUN *BEZA* is related to the verb *bozea*, one who cuts, rips or plunders (see Prov. 1:19). All gains derived from illegal or improper acts come under the category of *beza* (Gen. 37:26). A lover of *beza* is, by the very definition of this term, disqualified from holding a judicial post. Was there any need for an explicit disqualification of a lover of *beza* in the Torah?

It appears that it was in response to this question that the rabbis broadened the definition of *beza* to include acts which are deemed proper when practiced by ordinary citizens but improper for judges, who are subject to more exacting standards of probity and freedom from greed.

Most litigations involve claims and counterclaims which weaken the moral stance of a claimant, even if he wins. Sensitive people who refuse to litigate and consequently forgo their claims prove, according to Rabbi Joshua, their lack of greed.

Rabbi Eleazar posits a higher standard, hatred of money as proof of a lack of greed. This definition of *beza* is subject to challenge. It runs counter to the views of normative Judaism. We do not exalt vows of poverty nor honor people who hate money. Furthermore, the qualifier *anshe chayil,* mentioned in the same verse, is interpreted by Rabbi Joshua as "men of wealth."

Rabbi Elijah Gaon amends Rabbi Eleazar's comment by adding

39

the word *b'din* ("in court"); i.e., he hates litigation. This makes the definitions of both rabbis identical, even though they disagree throughout this passage.

To reconcile Rabbi Eleazer's view with mainstream Judaism, we must distinguish productive wealth from dormant wealth. It is proper to seek and love wealth for one's livelihood, or to use it to build up a community by providing employment, and of course to dispense charity. However, it is improper to hoard money, which serves no purpose except to give its owner the pleasure of seeing it grow. That amounts to loving money for its own sake. This, very likely, is the meaning of Rabbi Eleazer's definition, *sonei mamon azmom,* haters of money hoarded for its own sake. Such people are surely free from greed.

Slaves Who Love Their Masters

MISHPATIM

"And if the servant shall plainly say [amor yomar]" (Exod. 21:5). This repetition of the verb teaches us that his ear is not bored unless he declares twice: "I love my master" [ibid.] . . . and that his master loves him.

Mechilta, Exod. 21:5–6

THE HISTORY OF MANKIND, in the millennia preceding the establishment of democracy, is basically a chronicle of the oppression of the many by the few. Why did the human race tolerate tyranny for such a long time?

Intimidation was unquestionably a prime factor. However, force alone could not guarantee a tyrant's enduring sway. It was indoctrination, the ally of force, that induced popular docility. Submission to the king was declared a virtue, and obedience to him a religious imperative. The rise of the Hebrews against Pharaoh's enslavement was a sudden flash on a dark horizon. Their religion stripped tyrants of moral pretensions, and Judaism became the enemy of autocracy. Prophets denounced oppressive kings and rabbis defended laborers against the unlimited power of masters.

Under the tutelage of the rabbis, opposition to tyranny became part of the Jewish psyche. Any relationship between employer and employee that had even a remote resemblance to slavery was frowned upon. Laborers were given the right to terminate contracts, prior to their expiration, without incurring a penalty.

The portion of Mishpatim, which introduces the legislative part of the Torah, opens with the laws of Jewish indentured service. All societies have their quotas of misfits and criminals who are unable to cope on their own. According to rabbinic interpretation, the servant in this portion was a thief who, for lack of means, could not

41

make restitution for the value of the stolen goods. The court sells his services, and the proceeds are used to compensate the victim of the theft. Despite the fact that this servant is an undesirable individual, the rabbis must zealously protect his freedom even against himself.

A servant who wishes to extend his term of servitude must convince the court that he enjoys favorable conditions. His statement that he loves his master must be repeated twice to dispel any suspicion of the master's influence.

The bored ear is a symbol of the servant's socially maimed personality. The ear is bored because it heard God's injunction that "The children of Israel are My slaves" (Lev. 25:55), not slaves of slaves. One must say: "I love God my Lord," not "I love my master."

Religion and Nationalism

TERUMAH

*"And this is the offering which you shall take of them . . . rams'
skins dyed in red" [Exod. 25:3, 6]. Rabbi Judah said: "A large
clean beast was in the desert. It had a single horn (unicorn) on its
forehead, and its skin had six colors. They took it and made
curtains [from its skin]." Rabbi Nehemiah said: "It was a miracle.
[An animal] was created and hidden within the hour of its creation. . . . The length of each curtain was thirty cubits. How can one
procure a curtain of that length? But it was a miracle."*

Tanchuma, Exod. 25:3

THE ALLEGED SOURCES of the large curtains which covered the
exterior of the Tabernacle are as puzzling as the question to which
the two rabbis were responding. What is the significance of the
unicorn? Why did God order the procurement of material which
only a miracle could produce?

The Tabernacle was the first synagogue, the marvelous institution
which preserved Jewish identity through the ages. Two forces normally assure the perpetuation of a nation's distinctiveness, religion
and nationhood. However, the Jews in the desert, and later in the
diaspora, had to depend on religion alone to sustain their Jewish
identity.

All horned animals have two horns to defend themselves against
attack. These symbolize the two forces essential to a nation's survival. According to Rabbi Judah, the unicorn symbolized the single
spiritual force which has sustained the Jewish people through the
millennia. (Medieval Christianity also endowed the unicorn with
symbolic religious qualities.)

To Rabbi Nehemiah, the power of the synagogue to preserve
Jewish identity, even under most stressful conditions, remained a

43

mystery. He concluded that it was a miracle. Like the miraculous animal which was hidden soon after its creation, the synagogue's influence is hidden in some periods but never stops its influences.

Rabbis Judah and Nehemiah were survivors of the Hadrianic persecution. They witnessed the temporary decline of the synagogue and its triumphant resurgence after the fall of the tyrant. That inspired their enigmatic comments.

If these two rabbis were alive today, how would they react to the serious decline in the influence of the modern synagogue? Rabbi Judah most likely would express some anxiety but would deny any sense of despair. Rabbi Nehemiah would persist in his belief that the miraculous power of the synagogue is still at work, even though it appears to be hidden at the present time. After all, the age of miracles is not over. Witness the reestablishment of Israel and the *baal teshuvah* movement.

A Second Chance

"And this is the thing that thou shalt do unto them [Aaron and his sons] to hallow them to minister unto me" [Exod. 29:1]. Why did He choose Aaron and his sons for promotion and sanctity?

Tanchuma, Exod. 29:1

JACOB'S LAST TESTAMENT excluded Simon and Levi, and their descendants, from positions of leadership due to the violence of their tempers. In his ringing denunciation, he declared: "Cursed be their anger, for it was fierce. . . . I will divide them in Jacob [when Jews are under the foot of Esau] and scatter them in Israel [when Jews regain their freedom]." (Gen. 49:7). Yet the very tribe consigned by Jacob to anonymity was promoted by God to the status of religious leadership.

One cannot fault Jacob for penalizing his two sons. However, he could have softened the sting of his rebuke by commending their motives, even if their deeds were vile. They alone among the brothers could not contain a sense of outrage. It is sensitivity to evil which contributes most to the quality of a spiritual leader.

Jacob's fear that Levi's temper would become a dominant trait of his tribe was groundless. Aaron, a descendant of Levi, was a "lover and pursuer of peace" (Abot 1:12). Even under the pressure of Pharaoh's stubbornness, he did not lose his composure, in contrast to Moses, who once left Pharaoh "in hot anger."

Was Aaron tainted by his complicity in the golden calf affair? The Midrash wiped his slate clean. He acted in fear. "The Almighty bore no grudge against him in his heart" (Tanchuma, Exod. 29:1).

The midrashic discussion leaves a few questions for us to ponder. Should a hot temper bar an individual from holding public office? Should it disqualify lay and religious leaders of the Jewish community?

The total exoneration of Aaron after the golden calf affair puts into question the fairness of modern laws which mandate the preservation of criminal records of former prisoners even after they have paid their debt to society. This prevents their reintegration into society. It would be more appropriate to have special commissions designated to evaluate the rehabilitation of former prisoners, and if the commission's report is favorable, the public should be denied knowledge of the existence of such a record.

Prosperity of the Wicked

KI TISA

And he said: "Show me Thy glory" [Exod. 33:18]. He [Moses] asked to be informed on the subject of the reward of the righteous and the prosperity of the wicked. . . . What was the Almighty's response? "My presence shall not be seen" [ibid. 33:23].

Shemot Rabbah 45

MOSES ACQUIRED HIS knowledge of God in successive stages, beginning with God's revelation at the burning bush and continuing up to the dialogue following the golden calf incident. He learned that God was committed to the liberation of the Jewish people from bondage and to their settling in the land of Canaan (Exod. 3:8), that the Egyptian oppressor would be punished and an ongoing relationship established between God and His people (ibid. 6:6–7), that the wicked are punished and the righteous rewarded (ibid. 20:5–6), that God's protection of His people is conditioned upon obedience to His will (ibid. 23:22).

The disclosure of God's intent to destroy the Jewish people elicited Moses' request: "Show me thy ways" (ibid. 33:13). Like Abraham before him, he protested the destruction of the innocent with the guilty (Yalkut 392). Moses was assured that no decree emanating from God would hurt the innocent. Of course, this assurance does not prevent individuals, exercising their free will, from attacking the innocent. Witness the unprovoked attack of Amalek.

Moses' next request was a clarification of the anomaly of the wicked who prosper and the righteous who suffer, "Show me thy glory" (Exod. 33:18, Shemot Rabbah 45, Yalkut 395). The question of the suffering of the righteous and the rewards of the wicked raised by Kohelet (8:14) was attributed by the rabbis to Moses. According to a rabbinic consensus, the righteous are rewarded in

47

the hereafter (when their life's record has been completed). As for the prosperity of the wicked, God told Moses: "I will be gracious to whom I wish to be gracious" (Exod. 33:19) i.e., even if people deem them undeserving (Yalkut 395). In their eyes "My presence will not be seen" (Exod. 33:23).

Few people realize that in most instances it is man, not God, who is to blame for the anomaly of righteous who suffer and wicked who prosper. Let me cite but one illustration. Driven by need or greed, numerous people are lured by charlatans who recklessly promise high yields of profit, only to rob the entrusted capital. As a result they prosper. The honest broker, who plays by the rules, attracts few investors. As a result he suffers.

Unearned Reputations

VAYAKHEL

And Moses said unto the children of Israel: "See, the Lord has called by name Bezalel" [Exod. 35:30]. In the words of Kohelet: "A good name is better than precious oil" [7:1]. Why did he not say better than precious wine? [He mentioned oil] because when [water] is added to oil it floats on top, but [water] blends with all other liquids and is absorbed by them.

Tanchuma, Vayakhel 1

MOSES WANTED TO inform the Jews that it was God who had chosen Bezalel. He should have said, "God has called Bezalel. The phrase "by name" is superfluous. The rabbis inferred that the phrase was deliberately inserted to focus attention on the significance of a "good name" (or reputation). God's choice of Bezalel was based on his excellent reputation as a skilled craftsman.

This interpretation evolved into a broad-ranging discussion of the various sources which establish reputations. There was also an analysis of the relative reliability of these sources and a conclusion that some entrenched reputations are open to challenge.

The rabbis traced three sources from which reputations emanate. "One finds that a man may be known by three names. One is the name by which father and mother call their child" (Tanchuma, Vayakhel 2). Parents establish a child's reputation passively and actively. It is common knowledge that famous people lend some of their prestige to their children. However, a reputation established by osmosis has no substance. Parents also actively promote the reputation of their children, but parental judgment is flawed by a lack of objectivity.

"Another name is one by which the community calls an individual" (ibid.). Reputations established by a community carry more weight than a reputation promoted by parents; nevertheless these too are open to challenge. Communities are notoriously fickle in their judgments, and their motivation is frequently suspect. Public opinion is much too often slanted by prejudice or colored by favoritism. The man who follows the crowd is an instantaneous hero. One who resists is automatically rated a villain.

"Still another name is the one which an individual acquires for himself [as a result of a meritorious life]. The best of them is the one which he acquires for himself" (ibid.).

Reputations established by posterity, based on one's record, last forever. One who lives a decent life, and stands up for justice even in defiance of the mob, will earn the laurels of those who follow.

A Testimony to God's Presence

PEKUDE

"These are the accounts of the Tabernacle, the Tabernacle of Testimony" [Exod. 38:21]. It bears testimony to all nations that there was a reconciliation between God and the Israelites. How did this come about? It was Moses' defense which led to a reconciliation. Yet Moses was apprehensive. Who would inform the nations that God had forgiven Israel? God reassured him. "Go tell them [the Jews] 'Let them make Me a Sanctuary and I will dwell among them'" [ibid. 25:8]. The Tabernacle was therefore named "Tabernacle of Testimony" to testify to the presence of God among the Israelites.

Tanchuma, Pekude 1

WHEN MOSES LEARNED of the impending destruction of the Jews, he argued that the Egyptians would spread the word that God had rejected the Jews and brought them out of Egypt to annihilate them in the desert (ibid. 32:12). Moses feared that the libel, though false, would reverberate through the ages. God put him at ease: "The Tabernacle will testify that I dwell among them."

True, the pagan nations never picked up the calumny that God had rejected the Jews, but Christianity did. The author of the Midrash lived in the Christian era and was fully aware of the potentially frightening consequences of this libel. He attributed his concerns to Moses and, like him, looked to the synagogue to bear witness to the falsity of this charge. The extraordinary power of the synagogue to preserve Judaism in the face of cruel oppression is indisputable proof that God supports and blesses it.

Another passage in this Midrash shifts the focus from the power of the synagogue to its pleasant environment and healing influence, enabling Jews to retain a sense of community, pride, and human

51

dignity at a time when the authorities did their utmost to reduce them to the status of tolerated animals. This psychological phenomenon refuted the canard of God's rejection of the Jews.

The Midrash illustrates this point with a romantic parable. A king once left his beloved queen in a sudden fit of anger. The people were sure that he would never return. When he came back to dine with the queen, they said he would not stay. However, when a pleasantly perfumed aroma wafted from the palace, they admitted that there had been a reconciliation.

Unlike the Tabernacle of Testimony, the synagogue failed to convince its enemies that God dwells within it. Only the guilt of the Holocaust pressured the Second Vatican Council to retract the fundamental Christian belief that God had rejected the Jews. Regrettably, this belated confession of error has as yet failed to erase the latent hatred which is entrenched in the hearts of many people. We also regret that even after the Vatican's disavowal, we still need a Tabernacle of Testimony to testify to the many Jews who no longer see the presence of God in the synagogues of our day.

VAYIKRA

Blind Faith

"And the Lord called unto Moses" [Lev. 1:1]. It is written: "Bless the Lord, you His angels; you mighty in strength that fulfill his words. Hearkening unto the voice of His words and obeying His laws" [Ps. 103:20]. "His angels" is a reference to Moses and Aaron, who were called Malachim [messengers]. . . . Rav Acha said: "The psalmist refers to the Israelites because he describes those who fulfill God's words even before hearkening [understanding]. This [description] parallels the response of the Israelites: 'We shall do and we shall hearken' [Exod. 24:7]." Rabbi Yitzchak b. Nafcha says: "It refers to Jews who observe the sabbatical year."

Tanchuma, Vayikra 1

GOD'S CALL WAS interpreted by the Midrash as a command to Moses to continue his leadership. It appears that Moses had contemplated resigning his post because his mission had been completed (Tanchuma, Vayikra 3), but God ordered otherwise. It is to leaders like Moses, modest and dedicated, that the psalmist addresses his tribute: "mighty in strength." Indeed, even the most revered leader needs great strength and willpower to persevere in the face of opposition and contention. The Midrash singles out Moses and Aaron, but all leaders share the praise.

Rav Acha felt that select leaders deserve praise but not the class as a whole. History has proven time and again that self-aggrandizement is the sole incentive of many leaders. If tribute is to be paid to a class it belongs to the people of Israel, who faithfully follow God and their leaders without questioning their motives.

Rabbi Yitzchak approved of blind faith in God but saw blind faith in a leader as a slavish and self-destructive attitude. "We shall do and we shall hearken" is an inappropriate response to a human leader. The tribute of "mighty in strength" does not apply to all of society but only to those who act in accordance with the principle of the sabbatical year. The world and its wealth belong to God, who gave custody to man to manage it for the common good.

During a sabbatical year a landlord stands by and watches as "his farm is turned over to the public, his trees are out of his control, his fences are breached and his produce is eaten up. Yet he restrains his urge to speak out" (ibid. 1). Such people fully deserve the psalmist's tribute: "mighty in strength."

The laws of the sabbatical year are restricted to the land of Israel. Even the soil of Israel had to be taught a lesson in social responsibility. Land beyond the border was exempt from the laws of the sabbatical year. However, the spirit of these laws has universal application, binding on all who believe in God.

A Perception of the Messianic Age

TZAV

Rabbis Pinechas, Levi, and Jonathan quoted Rabbi Menachem of Galia: "In time to come [the messianic age] all sacrificial offerings will be discontinued, except for the thanksgiving offering (todah). All prayers will be discontinued, except for the prayers of thanksgiving.

Vayikra Rabbah 9

THERE IS NO DETAILED description in the Bible or Talmud of social conditions in the messianic era. Popular visions of that period, based on prophetic declarations, list the following as goals of the Messiah: the unification of the Jewish people, their restoration to their homeland, and the rebuilding of the Temple. He will spread the knowledge of God among the nations and arbitrate their conflicts. Weapons of war will be destroyed and no nation will resort to force.

No supernatural occurrences are envisioned by the talmudic sage Samuel: "This world differs from the messianic age only with regard to the servile conditions of the Jews in the diaspora" (Sanhedrin 91b). The social ills of society will continue. Samuel mentions the prevalence of poverty. By implication, such ills as physical sickness, envy, greed, and vindictiveness will also continue to plague society. Man will still be endowed with a free will to pursue evil, if that is his choice.

A more radical vision is implied in the Midrash in the superscription above which declares that only offerings and prayers of thanksgiving will continue in the messianic age. Only an end to poverty, sickness, sin, and crime can bring about a social order in which there will be no need for invoking God's forgiveness, help, and protection. It portrays an angel-like race which will no longer be endowed with free will.

Traditionalists view the Messianic age as the culmination of a gradually evolving process of many stages. This was confirmed in the Talmud by Rabbi Chiya the elder. "The redemption of Israel will proceed a little at a time. The more it progresses, the faster its pace" (Jer. Berachot 1:1). The Purim story was used as a blueprint. First stage: "Mordecai sat at the king's gate" (2:21). Second stage: "Then Haman took the apparel and the horse" (6:11). Third stage: "And Mordecai returned to the king's gate" (6:12). Fourth stage: "And Mordecai went forth from the king's gate in royal apparel" (8:15). Final stage: "The Jews had light and gladness" (8:16). Interestingly, Haman's threat in the interval between the first and second stages did not stop the progress of the process of redemption.

The stages of the redemption may be initiated by Jews or even by mankind. The establishment of Israel successfully achieved an important stage. The establishment of the United Nations to secure universal peace could have achieved another stage. Unfortunately, it shed the prophetic vision by turning into a forum for international hate-mongering.

When Joy and Sadness Blend

SHEMINI

"And it was on the eighth day" [Lev. 9:1]. Moses had instructed Aaron: "You shall not go out from the door of the Tent of Meeting seven days" [ibid. 8:33], "and at the door of the Tent of Meeting should sit day and night" [ibid. 8:35]. Moses was alluding [to an observance of shivah *prior to the deaths in the family of Aaron and his children.*

Tanchuma, Shemini 1

THE RESTRICTIONS IMPOSED on Aaron and his sons in the course of their consecrations were not unlike the ritual restrictions for mourners. They were ordered to sit seven days in their quarters and not to go outdoors during that period. In effect a ritual not unlike *shivah* was observed prior to the death of Nadav and Avihu. The Midrash points to a similar situation when God ostensibly observed seven days of mourning before the beginning of the flood (Gen. 7:4). Whereas God knew why he mourned, "they [Aaron and his sons] observed [*shivah*] but did not know why."

Mourners are confined to their homes to avoid being distracted from their concentration on their loss and the merit of the deceased. Induction into leadership is another occasion which calls for concentration—on the responsibilities of leadership and one's capacity to lead. Thus the Midrash portrays the consecration ritual as a melange of joy and sadness.

The concurrence of happiness and grief is not alien to human experience. Indeed many happy occasions contain the seeds of future sorrows. Joyous birthday celebrations, marking another year of life, also mark the diminution by a year of the span of one's life expectancy. Wedding celebrations, which mark the establishment of a marital bond, also plant the seeds of the grief that will eventuate when the bond is inevitably dissolved. Little did Aaron realize at the time of his consecration that his induction into the priesthood would be the cause of his children's death.

Ecclesiastes declares that there is "time to weep and a time to laugh" (3:4). Unfortunately, due to human lack of prescience, men occasionally weep and laugh at the wrong time. Who is the man who has never misjudged a good event for a bad one, and vice versa? God deplored man's acquired knowledge of good and evil (Gen. 3:22). Man's awareness of good and evil was not the problem. It was rather his potential for confusing the two.

Ancient Jewish folklore depicts Asmodeus, chief of demons, as contemptuous of humans because they are impressed by appearances rather than reality. When he saw a wedding procession he wept. When he heard a man order a pair of shoes that would last seven years, he laughed. The demon knew that the groom would die within the month and the shoe buyer had only seven days of life ahead of him (Gittin 68b).

When Silence Is Not Golden

TAZRIA

"And the priest shall look at the plague in the skin [to determine whether it is leprous]" [Lev. 13:3]. It was taught: "One sees [examines] all plagues except one's own plagues."

Vayikra Rabbah 15

IT IS CONSIDERED IMPRUDENT for physicians to diagnose their own illnesses and for lawyers to act as their own attorneys. Kohanim were licensed to diagnose leprosy but were forbidden to examine themselves. Rabbi Meir extended this prohibition to include the examination of close relatives.

The kohen was not under suspicion that he might deliberately cover up his findings. There is a valid assumption, however, that man's judgment, despite sincere efforts at objectivity, is subconsciously colored by self-interest. This is implied in the rabbinic dictum that "one sees other people's plagues but not one's own." However, this dictum also conveys another message beyond its halachic implication: "Man sees other people's faults but not his own."

People in distress habitually seek to blame others. Very few will admit to having contributed to their misfortune. One hears the laments of parents whose child has intermarried. They deserve our sympathy. However, what is disturbing is their self-exoneration, claiming that the child is rebellious or got involved with the wrong friends. At no time is there an expression of mea culpa. It never crosses their minds that a failure to raise the child in a positive Jewish atmosphere or to provide a substantial religious education might have contributed to their child's intermarriage. There are other instances in which failures on the part of decent citizens lessen the force of their sense of outrage. Citizens complain in private about the dishonesty of some officials. They resent in private hypocritical communal attitudes and prejudices against religious or racial minorities in their midst. They denounce in private rampant corruption and extortion. At no time, however, do these citizens raise their voices in public to protest the evil. They have a clear perception of other people's faults but do not see their own faults, their silence in the face of a miscarriage of justice.

The talmudic sages condemned those who are in a position to protest evil but fail to do so. The sages considered them as guilty as if they had participated in the perpetration of the evil. They made an exception, however, in situations where corruption is so endemic that protests would be of no avail. Thus Lot was saved in Sodom despite his failure to speak out against crime.

God intended to save the pious Jews of Jerusalem before its fall to the enemy. He deferred, however, to the heavenly prosecutor, who objected on the ground that they had remained silent in the face of unbridled lawlessness. Sadly, no one was saved (Tanchuma, Tazria 9).

Sickness Without Sin

METZORA

"And the priest shall go forth out of the camp [to examine the quarantined leper]" [Lev. 14:3]. Only a priest who may live in the camp is authorized to declare a leper clean. A leprous priest is disqualified.

Yalkut, Metzora 559

NUMEROUS ILLNESSES AFFLICT mankind. Most of them are not regarded as a heavenly punishment for a specific violation. A pious sufferer is advised to probe his past to discover whether he has committed a sin for which he may be punished and thus is in need of penance. If he finds no sin, he may conclude that his sickness is a natural occurrence, without any religious significance (Berachot 5a). He should pray for God's help to speed his recovery. When he recovers he need not perform a penitential ritual.

Leprosy, on the other hand, is considered a punishment for indulging in derogatory gossip. The rabbis pointed to Miriam, who had been afflicted with leprosy for the sin of gossiping (Num. 12:1). The Hebrew term *metzora* ("leper") is divisible into its component parts, *motzi-shem-ra*, "one who spreads rumors of a bad reputation." Furthermore, a cured leper was required to bring a guilt-offering. Clearly, he had been guilty of a sin. All of this reflected a link between gossip and leprosy. Gossip spreads quickly and affects many people. The same is true of leprosy.

Even the law regulating the incidence of the leprosy that attaches itself to some stones in a wall of a house was motivated, according to the Midrash, by an intent to expose a shortcoming of human character. The rabbis offered the following illustration: "A man begs his friend to lend him some wheat. The friend selfishly refuses, falsely claiming that he has no wheat in his house. God punishes him by having some leprosy cells attach themselves to his wall. The priest will remove the affected stones and, pending a final diagnosis, will order that all the vessels in the house be put outdoors. As a result, the hidden wheat is exposed to public view and the owner's lie is revealed." A gossiper believes that he can hide behind the shelter of anonymity and the wheat owner felt safe in the shelter of his home. Both are exposed in the end.

Every kohen is authorized to examine lepers, including kohanim who are ignorant and must depend on the help of experts. This right was denied to a leprous kohen, an exposed gossiper, and an insensitive person, for their diagnosis will be tainted by flawed judgment and character. In the choice between an ignorant and a corrupt judge, the Torah obviously prefers the former.

Those Who Question Heaven's Justice

ACHARE-MOT

"And the Lord spoke unto Moses after the death of the two sons of Aaron" [Lev. 16:1]. It was written: "All things come alike to all. There is one event to the righteous and to the wicked . . . as is the good so is the sinner . . . this is evil" [Eccles. 9:2–3]. "The good" refers to the sons of Aaron, "The sinners" refer to Korach and his mob, who were consumed by fire [Num. 16:35]. [Aaron's sons suffered the same fate (Lev. 10:22).]

Tanchuma, Achare-Mot 1

THE DEATH OF AARON'S SONS evoked conflicting midrashic reactions. The above-quoted author did not justify their death. He cited the comment of Koheleth that in the world is an "evil."

Is criticism of heaven compatible with piety? There are precedents in the Bible in which man's right of criticism is not denied. Abraham challenged God's justice in his plea for Sodom and was not reproached (Gen. 18:25). Job defiantly upheld his right to voice his complaints (7:11) and rejected the accusation that he was guilty of blasphemy. Indeed, God never rebuked him for his remarks.

On the other hand, most midrashic commentators, reflecting mainstream rabbinic thought, refused to criticize the punishment of Aaron's sons. It was therefore necessary to discover some offenses of which they were guilty. They suggested the following: (a) A failure to consult Moses before they declared the legality of the "strange fire" (Lev. 10:1). Graduate students were not permitted to declare new laws without consulting the faculty. This was probably intended to preclude radical innovations. (b) Aaron's sons had never married because they felt that no woman was good enough for them. (c) They looked forward to the death of Moses and Aaron so that they would replace them (Tanchuma, Achare-Mot 6).

The majority opinion refused to label the death of the sons an "evil." Mortal man is in no position to challenge God. The real purpose behind many events in this world may escape man because of his lack of comprehension. He must therefore submit to the will of God in the knowledge that whatever God does "is for the best."

Despite the opposition to the voicing of complaints against God, this continuing practice has served a good purpose by providing a safety valve for the release of pent-up grief. The recitation of the poem known as the Kaddish of Rabbi Levi Yitzchak of Berdichev, "A Din-Tore Mit Got," with all its reproaches addressed to God, met with enthusiastic applause in the shtetl. It skirted blasphemy by couching its phraseology in the form of a plea without reflecting a spirit of rebelliousness.

In Search of Holy Nations

KEDOSHIM

"Speak unto the entire congregation of the children of Israel and say unto them: 'You shall be holy, for I the Lord your God am holy'" [Lev. 19:2]. It is written: *"The Lord of Hosts is exalted through justice, and the Holy One is sanctified by righteousness"* [Isa. 5:16]. Rabbi Simon b. Yochai said: *"God will be exalted when He judges the wicked [nations]. [Rabbi Simon, a survivor of Hadrian's persecutions, was referring to Rome.]*

This chapter [Kedoshim] was part of the reading of Hakhel [when the festival pilgrims assembled to hear the king read biblical selections].

Vayikra Rabbah 24

HOLINESS, IN THE LEXICON of all religions, represents the highest state of perfection. The potential for holiness was granted to the Jewish nation as a whole, not to any individual. The injunction "you shall be holy" was addressed to the "entire congregation." The same was true of a previous injunction: "And you shall be a kingdom of priests and a holy nation" (Exod. 19:6).

The Midrash emphasizes the association of holiness with the nation by stating that the portion of Kedoshim was read by the king to the nation. How could a nation attain holiness? According to the Bible (Num. 15:40), the observance of all of God's commandments leads to holiness.

There have been many perfect individuals in this world. However, history has no record of any perfect nation. A national breach of the standards of law and ethics that guide individuals is generally considered proper, acceptable, and patriotic, so long as it advances a nation's interest. It is for this reason that God invested a just and lawful nation with holiness. Ezra urged the reconstituted Jewish

67

nation to attain holiness so that "God will be sanctified through you in the eyes of the nations" (20:4). Alas, God was not exalted in the eyes of those nations who wantonly murdered Jews throughout the diaspora. That will happen only when God "judges the wicked nations" (Vayikra Rabbah 24).

No biblical hero was ever called holy. Moses and Samuel were each entitled "man of God" (Deut. 33:1; I Sam. 9:10).

After the dispersion of the Jewish nation, attention was focused on individuals to designate those who were worthy of the crown of holiness. In the talmudic period that title was bestowed upon Rabbi Judah Hanasi (Sanhedrin 98b). The victims of the crusaders' massacres were enshrined as holy Jews. Subsequently, the masters of Kabbalah gained the crown, and the same has been the reward of Hasidic leaders.

There are many holy men among the nations of our time. We are still looking for a modern nation worthy of the crown of holiness.

Inaudible Voices

EMOR

"And the Lord said unto Moses: 'Speak unto the priests' " [Lev. 21:1] How is this verse relevant to the concluding verse of the preceding chapter, "A man or a woman that divines by a ghost or a familiar spirit shall be put to death" [ibid. 20:27]? God peered into the future and saw Saul's murder of the priests of Nov [I Sam. 22:18] and his subsequent inquiry of a ghost and familiar spirit [ibid. 28:7].

Tanchuma, Emor 2

THE TORAH PROHIBITS necromancy. People who are in need of advice and guidance are instructed to "speak unto the priests." The Midrash noted the irony of King Saul's predicament. He exterminated all diviners and practitioners of witchcraft in keeping with the biblical injunction. Tragically, he also killed the high priest and his associates at Nov. When he eventually needed advice, there was no high priest available for consultation. In desperation, he set out to find a diviner who might have been overlooked during the massacre.

King Saul's dilemma was by no means unique. There are many people who antagonize good friends and end up seeking the company of individuals who are enemies in disguise. There are many people who disdain the warnings of competent physicians and end up in the clutches of quacks.

Saul's distress was not relieved by his encounter with the ghost of Samuel. In addition to Saul there were present at that time Saul's companions and the woman diviner. The Midrash took note of the different reactions of the people who attended the seance. The necromancer saw the rising spirit but did not hear the sounds emanating from it. Saul heard sounds but saw no image. The companions neither heard nor saw anything. It follows, the Midrash concluded, that in all such instances the diviner sees images, the inquirer hears sounds, and bystanders are not aware of anything.

This midrashic comment does not necessarily reflect a belief in necromancy. According to Maimonides, ghosts cannot be made to appear at the command of a diviner. Saul was sadly taken in by a fraudulent make-believe performance.

There are other ways of raising the spirits of deceased scholars and leaders of the past. All one has to do is to recall their images in his mind and hear once again the sound of their words. The Midrash uses the episode involving Saul to depict the varying reactions of posterity to the spiritual legacy of the past. Some recall the image but hear no sounds and are unaffected. Others hear the sounds and are deeply influenced. Still others are not even aware of the existence of a spiritual legacy. One meets with the same type of reactions in response to the traditions which parents of every generation transmit to their offspring.

No-Fault Poverty

"And when your brother grows poor" [Lev. 25:25]. It is written: "Happy is he who is considerate of the poor [maskil el dol]. . . . *The Lord will deliver him on the day of evil" [Ps. 41:2].*

Vayikra Rabbah 34

JUDAISM CLASSIFIES THREE CATEGORIES of impoverishment: no-fault poverty, self-inflicted poverty, and penal poverty. The first is due to disability or circumstances beyond one's control. The second is due to negligence or a gambling habit. The third is in punishment for sin. Charity is called for in all categories of poverty.

Penal poverty, like penal pain, was inflicted shortly after the creation (Gen. 3:16, 18). No-fault poverty and self-inflicted poverty are endemic to human existence. Such is the biblical declaration: "For the poor shall never cease out of the land" (Deut. 15:11). All attempts to eradicate poverty on a national scale have failed.

The Bible indicates that poverty can be avoided by people who show consideration for the poor. Thus, those who observe the laws of the sabbatical year and wipe out debts accrued by debtors will be recipients of God's special blessing: "There shall be no needy among you, for the Lord shall surely bless you" (Deut. 15:4). The psalmist echoes this promise: "The Lord will deliver the *maskil el dol* on the day of evil" (Ps. 41:2).

What is the meaning of *maskil el dol*? Its most likely rendition is: "one who deals sensibly with the poor." The Midrash offers a variety of interpretations of this phrase in an ascending order of degrees of involvement with the poor (Vayikra Rabbah 34).

1. An individual whose positive instincts dominate his negative ones. This is addressed to a victim of self-inflicted poverty who must foreswear greed and get-rich-quick schemes. If he exercises self-restraint, God will help him.

71

2. One who gives a penny (*perutah*) to the poor. This demonstrates his concern for the poor, though it is of a minimal degree.

3. One who buries the body of an unknown Jew (*met-mitzvah*). This represents a greater involvement with the poor. No one is poorer than the dead.

4. One who helps a falsely accused individual to escape from hostile and vindictive authorities. The benefactor exposes himself to great risk and is surely deserving of God's blessing.

5. One who visits and attends to the sick. There was a desperate need for health-care assistance in ancient times. This was particularly true of poor patients. Those who volunteered their services had to overcome a psychological barrier. The very person for whom they risked their health was likely to be the one who would infect them with his disease.

Rules and Rationales

"If you walk in My statutes (chukkim), *and keep My command-ments, and do them" [Lev. 26:3]. Rabbi Chanina the son of Papa said: "If you observe the Torah, I will consider it as if you your-selves have made them [the commandments]. This is the sense of the phrase 'and do them.' "*

Yalkut 671

CHUKKIM ARE LAWS FOR which no reason is indicated nor can one perceive their rationale. There are some people who question the validity of such statutes and ignore them. To achieve greater compli-ance, God, according to the Midrash, promised that all who observe the *chukkim* will be rewarded as if they themselves had instituted those laws. The apparent redundancy of the phrase "and do them" is thus fully explained.

Individuals who initiate legislation are inclined to obey it because it reflects their personal views. For this reason, citizens of a demo-cratic state, where representatives of the people enact legislation, are more likely to abide by the laws than citizens of a dictatorship, where laws are imposed and compliance is based on fear.

Chukkim have a place in a religious code. Man is incapable of fully understanding God and His ways, and hence is not expected to fully comprehend all His laws. However, there is no place for *chukkim* in a civil code.

If the citizenry is to accept civil laws, they must have a sound rationale. Therefore it is essential that the purpose of any given law or request be stated in comprehensible terms. This is true both of formal legislation and of private rules established by parents to guide their children.

An abundance of legislation is annually passed on the national,

73

state, and local levels. Only a minority of the people affected by these laws are aware of their purpose. Every law enacted by legislators should have a memorandum attached to it, stating its rationale and what it aims to achieve. This will assure a wider compliance. Signs on highways ordering a reduction in speed should always carry the slogan, "Your life is at risk if you exceed this limit."

All children are instructed to abide by some rules. Some children do not understand the reason behind these rules and will try to resist them. Bedtime restrictions are highly resented. Repeated parental explanations would ease the resentment.

Many children resist the burden of a Jewish education imposed on them in afterschool hours. Threats and force destroy the goal which this education is designed to achieve. The child's motivation must be constantly reinforced until he grasps the importance of his role as a young warrior in the battle for the survival of Jewish traditions.

BAMIDBAR

Solomon's Open-Door Policy

BAMIDBAR

"And the Lord said unto Moses . . . in the Tent of Meeting" [Num. 1:1]. Rabbi Joshua the son of Levi said: "If the nations of the world had been aware of the Temple's goodwill they would have protected it with surrounding walls. The sanctuary put gentiles in a more advantageous position than Jews. Thus Solomon prayed: 'Concerning the strangers who are not of Your people Israel . . . hear . . . and do according to all that the stranger implores You' [I Kings 8:41, 43]. However, with regard to Jews, he prayed as follows: 'Render unto every man according to all his ways' [II Chron. 6:30]," whatever he deserves."

Tanchuma, Bamidbar 3

KING SOLOMON ENVISAGED a stream of non-Jewish worshippers attracted by the fame of the Temple. He implored God to respond to all their prayers so that His glory would spread among the nations of the earth and they would come to fear Him. Such magnanimity is unprecedented in the world's religious literature.

As was noted in the Midrash, Solomon's proclamation of an open-door policy failed to produce the anticipated stream of non-Jewish worshippers. It was not until the emergence of the Jewish diaspora that interfaith contacts stimulated a trickle of pagan pilgrims to Jerusalem.

The international traffic increased when Judea came under Roman domination. An improved network of roads facilitated long-distance travel. A Roman garrison was quartered in the Antonia fortress, abutting the wall of the Temple court. Merchants and visitors came from Ethiopia, Macedonia, Parthia, Crete, and many parts of the Roman Empire. It was mainly trade, not religion, which brought them to Jerusalem.

77

The Roman authorities were antagonistic to the Temple because they viewed it as a symbol of Jewish political aspirations. The torching of the Temple in the year 70 did not violate their moral scruples.

Solomon's open-door policy was not reciprocated by medieval Christianity. A secret Jew who participated in the rites of the church was guilty of a capital offense. The midrashic comment about the failure of non-Jews to protect the Temple points up a paradox. Hatred of Judaism led to the razing of synagogues even when the attackers could have put the structures to good use. Spain expelled its Jews, disregarding its inevitable economic decline. The Nazis burned down synagogues despite the damage to their own economy. They diverted scarce rolling-stock to expedite the delivery of Jews to the gas chambers even though it also expedited the collapse of the military front in Russia. "If the nations of the world had only been aware of the Temple's goodwill . . ."

The Priestly Benedictions

NASO

"Thus shall you bless the children of Israel" [Num. 6:23]. The Almighty said: "Formerly I Myself used to bless My creatures" [Adam and Eve, Gen. 1:28; Noah and sons, ibid. 9:1; Abraham, ibid. 24:1]. After that God told Abraham: "You are authorized to deliver benedictions." That was the meaning of God's statement: "And may you be a blessing" [ibid. 12:2].

Tanchuma, Naso 9

FROM THE VERY BEGINNING God had revealed Himself to individuals, not to groups. The sole exception was the revelation on Mount Sinai, when all the people heard God's voice. Even then the Jews begged Moses to act as an intermediary between God and them (Exod. 20:16). Abraham was the first person authorized by God to compose and deliver his own benedictions. The same right was also granted to Isaac, Jacob, and Moses (Gen. 27:30, 48:15; Deut. 33:1). Their benedictions were framed in the context of a prayer to God (Gen. 27:28).

The opening of the *ohel-moed* (Num. 7:1) marked the establishment of the first Jewish house of prayer. Henceforth Jews would gather there to atone for their sins and to solicit God's blessing. Provision had to be made for the delivery of daily benedictions, even in the absence of a leader authorized to compose and pronounce official blessings. To meet this need God introduced the Priestly Benedictions (Num. 6:23).

The choice of priests for the performance of this task was not based on their personal merit. There were some among them who had little education. They were chosen because they were in charge of the religious functions of the sanctuary and were always available to perform a service.

The permanent text of the benedictions was fixed by God. The priests could not change the wording nor even render them in a foreign language. To ensure accuracy, each word of the blessings was recited first by a prompter and then repeated by the priests. It was not the priests who blessed the people, but "I [God] who will bless them" (ibid. 6:27).

Can an ancient text meet the needs of people who live in a different era under changed conditions? Yes. With the exception of "Peace," the only specific benediction which is always timely, the other benedictions are vague. Their flexibility allows for multiple interpretations to meet all exigencies.

Which midrashic interpretations would suit most the needs of modern American Jewry? I suggest the following: "May God bless you" (economically, Yalkut 710); "preserve you" (physical security, ibid.); "shine His countenance" (children who will seek the enlightenment of Torah, ibid.); "be gracious unto you" (to find grace in the eyes of society and the authorities, Tanchuma, Naso 10); "lift up His face" (that we face God directly and not look at Him askance, ibid.); "grant you peace" (within and without).

The Menorah Outshines the Altar

BEHA'ALOTECHA

"When you light the lamps" [Num. 8:2]. Eleven tribes brought offerings [to dedicate the altar] but the tribe of Levi brought none. . . . Aaron feared that he was to blame for the exclusion of the tribe of Levi, so God instructed Moses to tell Aaron: "Have no fear. You will perform a function of greater importance [the lighting of the menorah]. Sacrifices are brought only when the Temple is in existence, but the lights are forever. The same is true of the benedictions which you recite when blessing My children. They will never be discontinued."

Tanchuma, Beha'alotecha 5

THE SMALL MENORAH, by comparison with the massive altar, must have appeared insignificant to Aaron. Not only physically but functionally as well, the altar had a greater claim to prominence. It was the principal medium for man's communion with God. However, Moses pointed out that the altar was an adjunct of the Temple without which it could not exist. The menorah was an independent entity, its function transcending time and space.

According to Rabbi Eleazar, the altar served four objectives: the cancellation of evil decrees, the granting of national prosperity, the endearment of the people to God, and atonement for man's sins (Ketubot 10b). Its primary goal was rehabilitation, to undo the consequences of sin so that man might remain dear to God and deserve His continued blessings.

On the other hand, the main objective of the Menorah was preventability, to inform man of the distinction between right and wrong and to keep him from lawlessness. Its light symbolized Torah and education.

81

The task of perpetuating Judaism was assigned to the priests, who assumed the professional role of teachers. Their instructions had a greater impact on the Judaic character of the developing nation than did their priestly service related to the sacrificial rites. To love God and to love all men is a tribute to man's dignity and strength. To forgive man's sins and wrongs is a concession to his weakness. Aaron was excluded from dedicating the altar to stress the greater significance of his teaching assignment.

The destruction of the Temple diminished the role of the priesthood. The altar was replaced by prayers as the principal means of communing with God. Except for the formal recitation of the Priestly Benedictions, prayers to God have become the personal obligation of every Jew. As for the lights of the menorah, the eternal symbols of the enlightenment of the Torah, a prominent role has been delegated to women. It reflects the essential and critical part played by women in implanting a love of tradition in the hearts of the very young.

Is An Honest Misjudgment Punishable?

SHELACH

"Send some men that they may spy out the land of Canaan" [Num. 13:2]. [The spies] were great men . . . they were esteemed by the Jews and Moses as men of virtue [tzadikim]. Yet Moses did not rely on his own judgment regarding their merit. He consulted the Almighty and obtained God's approval of each selection. It was only after the forty days [of spying] that the men became turncoats and precipitated the evil decree [barring that generation from entering Canaan].

Yalkut, Shelach 742

WAS THE SEVERE PUNISHMENT of the Jews warranted? The report of the spies answered Moses' inquiries and presented an accurate account of what they had observed. Only their judgmental assessment of the feasibility of an invasion was a disappointment to God and to Moses. Is the expression of an honest opinion by honest men a punishable offense?

A dissenting Midrash presents a different view. The spies, according to this rabbi, were wicked men who all along had favored a return to Egypt. God had never approved of the spying expedition because it betrayed a distrust of His earlier promise: "The Lord your God brings you into a good land, a land of brooks and water" (Deut. 8:7). The negative assessment of the spies was deliberately slanted by their bias, and thus they deserved to be punished. There is, however, a question that remains to be answered. Why did God permit a group of wicked men to proceed with the spying expedition?

Both midrashic opinions are acceptable if we place the episode of the spies within the context of mutual testing which marked the

83

relationship of God and the Jewish people. The Jews tested God (Num. 14:22) and God tested the Jews (Deut. 8:2).

The Jews were about to enter Canaan to found an independent Jewish nation. It was essential to test their capacity at that moment to prove that they were ripe for the task. In a similar situation, Abraham, the father of the Jewish people, was also tested prior to his entry into the land of Canaan and the Philistines. It is said that he was tested ten times (Abot 5:4). The third test was given to him to prove his willingness to submit to God's command to move to a new land. Even the location of the destination was withheld.

If the invasion of Canaan was to succeed, the Jews had to prove that they were strongly motivated by their faith in God and would not retreat even in the face of great danger. They failed the test and were barred because they had proved their lack of proper motivation and zeal. No punishment was involved.

The first Midrash conveys a subtle message. Even those who are *tzadikim* under normal circumstances may lose their nerve and faith under life-threatening conditions.

Korach's Four Points of Contention

KORACH

*"God has separated you [Korach] from the congregation of Israel"
[Num. 16:9]. Moses said: "God has instituted separateness in the
process of creation. He has separated light from darkness [Gen.
1:4] . . . for the good of the world. For the same reason He has
separated the Jews from other nations [Lev. 20:26]. Aaron was
separated [from the tribe of Levi] that he might be sanctified as
most holy [I Chron. 23:13]. You cannot mix light and darkness,
which God has set apart, nor can you mix the other [separations]."*

Bamidbar Rabbah 18

WHAT MOTIVATED KORACH'S REBELLION? The Midrash suggests
a number of reasons: theological disagreements; the notion that
Moses was guilty of self-aggrandizement and nepotism; resentment
of deteriorating conditions in the desert; and opposition to the
creation of a hereditary caste of priests (Tanchuma, Korach 1–3, 7).

The Bible mentions only the fourth objection: ". . . the entire
congregation is holy, why do you exalt yourselves above the congregation of the Lord?" (Num. 16:3). Korach advocated an egalitarian
society without a priestly caste based on birth. Moses did not
respond to the proposal on its merits, for he knew that Korach's
agitation was motivated by self-interest.

The Midrash fills the gap by addressing the issue raised by Korach. Its rebuttal formulates several principles. Separateness was
sanctioned by God at the beginning of creation. Separateness is not
based on the superiority of the separated part. It is dictated by a
desire to produce an improvement "for the good of the world." The
mixture of light and darkness served no useful purpose. After their

85

separation each of the elements became useful, the day for work and the night for rest.

God separated the Jews from other nations to expedite the acceptance of monotheism by mankind. The separation was done "for the good of the world." The superiority of any one nation was not a factor.

The Midrash does not discuss the merit of a hereditary priestly caste. Apparently, it felt that the need for one was quite obvious. All creeds have occasionally experienced a shortage of priests. The numerous rituals performed at the Temple required the service of numerous priests. Only a hereditary caste of priests could meet this great demand. Furthermore, the priests had no territory of their own and had no stake in intertribal squabbles. This prevented the creation of a politicized priesthood.

There was no hereditary caste of scholars and teachers. Elijah, Jeremiah, Ezekiel, and Zechariah were of priestly descent, but they were outnumbered by the prophets who descended from other tribes. Needless to say, priestly descent was no factor in the appointment of the great teachers and scholars of the Talmud.

A Non-Pacifist Religion of Peace

CHUKAT

"And Israel sent messengers to Sichon, king of the Amorites. . . .
Let me pass through your land" [Num. 21:21–22]. [Israel acted in
the spirit of the verse: "Depart from evil and do good, seek peace
and pursue it" [Ps. 34:15]. Normally, one is not required to go in
search of mitzvot. For instance, the mitzvah of sending away a
dam sitting upon its young [Deut. 22:6–7] does not devolve until
one "chances upon a bird's nest". . . . However, the mitzvah of
peace is different. One must search for it in his own location and
pursue it elsewhere. That is why "Israel sent messengers [of
peace]."

Tanchuma, Chukat 22

OUR DAILY LITURGY PROCLAIMS GOD "a sovereign Lord of all peace." The Priestly Benedictions (Num. 6:24) conclude with a prayer for peace. King Solomon composed a special prayer: "Let there be an abundance of peace till the moon be no more" (Ps. 72:7). According to the Talmud, individuals who promote peace between man and his fellow are rewarded by God in this world and in the hereafter (Shabbat 127a). Surely, the reward must be even greater for those who promote peace between nations.

The psalmist's exhortation, "Depart from evil and do good, seek peace and pursue it," had a great impact on Christianity. This verse is quoted verbatim in the Christian Testament, albeit no credit is given to its author (I Peter 3:11).

The prophetic promise of a golden age of peace "at the end of days" is one of the most inspiring messages of the ancient sacred literature. Isaiah's vision of a period when nations "shall beat their swords into ploughshares and their spears into pruning forks;

87

nation shall not lift up sword against nation, neither shall they learn war any more" (2:4) has become the most desired goal of modern mankind.

Judaism is a non-pacifist religion of peace. It recognizes that some wars are justifiable. When Sichon, the king of the Amorites, barred the passage of the Israelites over a road traversed by international traffic, despite iron-clad pledges of nonaggression, war was the only alternative. When ancient and modern Amalekites pursue terrorist policies which threaten innocent nations, war may be the only recourse left to the peaceful nations of the world. Of course self-defensive wars have always been considered legitimate.

"Peace" was a household word in ancient Israel. It was with "peace" that they greeted each other and bade farewell to one another. Interestingly, the word "peace" appears in the Bible more than 220 times, compared with thirteen times in the Christian Testament and three times in the Koran.

Incidentally, peace, according to the Talmud, is in the same class with charity. It has to be pursued (Shabbat 127a).

A Master of Ambivalence

"And God said to Balaam: 'Do not go with them [Balak's messengers]' [Num. 22:12]. He [Balaam] said to Him [God]: "So I will curse them right here." He said to him: "Do not curse the people [Israelites]." "In that case, I will bless them." He said to him: "They do not need your blessing. They are blessed already."

Tanchuma, Balak 6

The reported dialogue between God and Balaam raises some questions. If God did not approve of it, Balaam's curse would have been inconsequential. Why was it necessary to forbid his curses? In the midrashic version of the dialogue Balaam openly reveals his hatred of Jews. What prompted his reversal, the sudden offer to bless them? Why was his offer rejected?

According to Ibn Ezra, if Balaam had cursed the Jews, they would attribute all misfortunes that might befall them in the future to the effectiveness of his curses.

There is another explanation. Human curses are frequently self-fulfilling. The medieval church reviled and cursed Jews for centuries on end. This prepared the ground for the massacres during the Crusades and the bestiality of the Holocaust. Balaam's curses would have incited the enemies of the Jews to a higher pitch of barbaric ferocity.

Why did Balaam offer to bless the Jews, and why was he denied permission? The denial might have been intended as a warning to Jews: Beware of an enemy's blessing; it may be a curse in disguise.

Balaam was a master of the double-entendre. In his first parable he described Jews as a "people that shall dwell alone" (Num. 23:9). He appeared to be praising Jews as the only people capable of resisting the universal tide of paganism. In reality, he was branding

89

them for their exclusivity. The pagan anti-Semites of antiquity seized upon this charge to denounce Jews for their lack of sociability and friendly intercourse with their pagan neighbors.

The second part of Balaam's complimentary remark was even more flagrantly ambivalent: "And you shall not be reckoned among the nations" (ibid.). His apparent reference to Jewish resistance to assimilation had an authentic laudatory ring. However, what he had in mind was to deny Jews national status on an equal footing with other nations.

Charges of violations of human rights are leveled against many members of the United Nations. Israel is the only member threatened by some "friendly" speakers with the forfeiture of its right to national existence.

Zeal and Conciliation

*"Therefore say: 'I give unto him [Pinechas] My covenant of peace' "
[Num. 25:12]. Rabbi Ilaa said: "Pinechas was placed in the succession of high priesthood after he slew Zimri [ibid. 8]. It was
written: 'And it shall be unto him and his seed after him a
covenant of everlasting priesthood' " [ibid. 13]. Rav Ashi said:
"[The designation of Pinechas was made] after he promoted peace
between the tribes. It was said: 'And Pinechas the priest heard'
[Josh. 22:30]." [The honorific title "priest" was attached to his
name for the first time.]*

Yalkut, Pinechas 772

THE EROSION OF JEWISH COMMUNAL discipline dictated the appointment of a new and vigorous leadership. Pinechas had won his
laurels at Shittim and as a result was singled out for promotion. At
the same time Moses was ordered to prepare for the end of his career
(Num. 27:13).

Moses was concerned about the qualifications of his successor. As
he pondered the quality of Aaron's and his own leadership, it must
have occurred to him that Aaron was too meek and pliant while he
was too stern and rigid. Accordingly, he pleaded: "Let the Lord, the
God of the spirits of all flesh, set a man over the congregation" (ibid.
27:16). The term "spirits," according to the rabbis, referred to the
gamut of human tempers and dispositions. Moses begged for a
leader who would deal with each person on an individual basis, with
patience and understanding.

In Rabbi Ilaa's opinion Pinechas was chosen on the basis of his
decisive reaction to Zimri. However, what is proper in times of
emergency may not serve the interests of a community under normal
conditions.

The heads of the tribes reacted negatively to Pinechas' impulsiveness (Yalkut 771). The later rabbis also had their reservations. Acts motivated by excessive zeal are justified only in critical emergencies but not otherwise (Jer. Sanhedrin, end of chap. 9).

Unlike Rabbi Ilaa, Rabbi Ashi felt that the promotion of Pinechas was not due to the slaying of Zimri but rather to his later success as a conciliator and promoter of peace among the feuding Jewish tribes.

Talmudic lore identifies Pinechas with the prophet Elijah (Yalkut 771). The acclaim of both men was couched in the same terms. Pinechas turned away (*heshiv*) God's wrath (Num. 25:11). On the eve of the messianic era, Elijah will bring about (*veheshiv*) a reconciliation between the generations (Mal. 3:24). Elijah's ultimate distinction will not rest on his earlier role as a zealous critic of his people but on his subsequent role as a conciliator who unites parents and children in love and faith.

Benefactors and Beneficiaries

MATTOT

"Avenge the children of Israel of the Midianites" [Num. 31:2]. The Almighty ordered Moses to avenge the children of Israel . . . yet Moses sent others [to do God's bidding]. He considered it improper for him to cause them harm because he had spent his youthful years in Midian. To quote a fable: "Do not throw stones into a well which once gave you its water."

Tanchuma, Mattot 3

THE MIDRASH DISCUSSES an ethical dilemma. Beneficiaries are emotionally indebted to their benefactors and avoid hurting them. Does this moral restraint dissolve in the event that the benefactor has turned hostile in the interim?

The well in the fable had never lost its image of benevolence. Would the admonition remain in force even if the well's water had spilled over and flooded the man's property?

When Moses was ordered to strike the waters of the Nile, he delegated the task to Aaron (Exod. 7:19). "He refrained from striking the Nile because its water had at one time protected him" (ibid., Rashi). The Nile did not project a halo of innocence, having drowned many Jewish infants since then.

Moses, according to the Midrash, retained a sense of indebtedness to the Midianites despite their recent support of Moab's hostile plot.

It was not the intent of the Midrash to glorify Moses' high personal standard of ethical conduct. Its educational aim was to lay down moral guidelines for all Jews to follow.

The angels who rescued Lot cautioned him and his family not to look behind them at the flames which burned the people of Sodom. The apparent reason was to prevent them from gloating. The Sodomites were criminals who deserved their punishment. Yet Lot's reaction was to be subdued because of his indebtedness to the Sodomites for tolerating and protecting him.

The Torah similarly cautioned the Jewish people not to indulge in excessive hate of the Egyptians, who had caused them so much pain and agony. "Do not abhor an Egyptian, because you were a stranger in his land" (Deut. 23:8). They stopped short of genocide, and for that Jews must feel indebted.

In the amoral world of Nazidom there were shades and gradations of depravity. It is shocking that among the most villainous Nazi criminals were individuals who had been recipients of Jewish generosity and friendship. This was particularly common in Eastern Europe, where people who had been given access to Jewish homes and institutions were sometimes among the most brutal of the local collaborators. It was as if they were trying to silence a lingering sense of indebtedness by means of overwhelming savagery.

Perceiving God's Leadership

MASSEI

"These are the journeys of the children of Israel" [Num. 33:1]. It is written: "You led [nachita. Your people like a flock by the hands of Moses and Aaron [Ps. 77:21]. Nachiya is an acronym. [n, ch, y, and t are the initials of the following words:] nisim ["miracles"], chaim ["life"], yam suf ["Red Sea"], Torah. So says Rabbi Eliezer. According to Rabbi Joshua, [the words are:] niflaot ["wonders"], cherut ["freedom"], yemincha ["God's right hand"], teluyei rosh ["heads high"]. According to Rabbi [the words are:] nevi'im ["prophets"], chasaidim ["pious"], yesharim ["upright"], temimim ["perfect"], according to Rabbi Akiva, [the words are:] "noraot" (frightful things), "charon" (God's anger), "yadecha" (God's hand), "tehomot" (depths).

Tanchuma, Massei 2

THE THEME OF THE RABBINIC discussion, how to perceive God's leadership in times of stress, is linked to the portion of Massei, a record of early Jewish wanderings and unrest. The discussion was inspired by the word *nachita*, ("you [God] led"), which appears in the Book of Psalms. The same word also appears in the post-exodus song of Moses (Exod. 15:13). Moses uttered it in the euphoric moment of triumph, when it was easy to perceive divine leadership. The psalmist, however, perceived it even "in the days of stress" (77:3).

Rabbi Eliezer's acronym points to the miracles of the exodus, which should convince the people of God's eternal presence. Rabbi Joshua asserts the need for perceiving God in the present, not only in the past. The wonder of Jewish survival to this day is evidence of God's leadership. Jews have never again been enslaved since the exodus. They continued to live in freedom even under the oppressive

95

rule of Emperor Hadrian, without losing their sense of dignity and pride.

Rabbi Akiva was an activist who had backed Bar Kochba's rebellion. God, according to him, does not approve of meek submission to tyranny. The nation must oppose oppression with passion and anger, and offer resistance whenever possible. It is in their defiance and in God's invisible intervention that the people can perceive His leadership.

Rabbi was a pacifist who made accommodations to the Roman authorities. Resistance is foredoomed to failure and therefore is suicidal. It is sinful to sacrifice precious lives in a futile struggle. Yet God's leadership can still be perceived in the consistent quality of the Jewish people throughout Jewish history. Their prophets and scholars are a testimony to God.

Three of the discussing rabbis were present at the famous Seder at B'nai B'rak. There is little doubt that the aforementioned theme was one of the many topics which challenged their minds throughout the night until daybreak.

DEVARIM

Repetitious Rebukes

DEVARIM

"These are the words which Moses spoke unto all of Israel" [Deut. 1:1]. Are these the only words which Moses spoke? These [are in a special category], words of admonition.

Yalkut, Devarim 788

WORDS LEND THEMSELVES to various ends. Some heal, others bruise; some comfort, others irritate; some befriend, others antagonize; some approve, others reprove. Words at the disposal of a preacher are like the hypodermic needle in the hands of a physician. There are important distinctions, however. The effect of the injection is predictable. The effect of a preacher's admonition cannot be foretold in advance.

Moses was considered the preeminent preacher of the Jewish people. The verse in Proverbs, "He that rebukes a man shall in the end find more favor" (28:23), was interpreted as referring to Moses (Devarim Rabbah 1:1). He was rated so high because he possessed the qualifications of an effective preacher. His sincerity was beyond reproach, and he was motivated by love and concern for the people. Furthermore, the people were receptive to his criticisms (Sifri, Devarim 1:1).

The rabbis took to heart the caveat in Proverbs: "Reprove not a scorner, lest he hate you" (9:8). Rabbi Tarfon noted the absence of effective preachers in his generation due to the lack of popular receptiveness to rebukes. Similarly, Rabbi Eleazar b. Azariah noted the absence of qualified preachers in his generation (Sifri, Deut. 1:1).

Jacob and Moses chided no one until shortly before their deaths. They wanted to make sure that they would not get into the habit of repeating rebukes, for that would have provoked a negative reaction (Yalkut, Devarim 800).

Jacob's delayed rebuke of his son Reuben was explained by him as follows: "I was afraid that you [Reuben] would leave me and join my brother Esau" (Sifri, Devarim 1:3). Jacob's practical precaution was adopted by the rabbis. A reprover must make sure that his chiding will not turn out to be counterproductive and defeat the purpose of his admonition.

This important rabbinic advice has not been universally accepted. Some worshippers complain about a barrage of weekly sermons of rebuke. What makes this practice more objectionable is the fact that the worshippers are not really the targets of the fulminating sermons. Those to whom the preacher's words are addressed are not present at the service to hear it. Seasoned preachers know that teaching sermons, without the sting of a reprimand, are in the long run more effective in attaining results. The real purpose of Deuteronomy was to repeat previous instructions so that they would gradually sink in.

An Appearance of Injustice

VA'ETCHANAN

"And I besought the Lord" [Deut. 3:23]. It is written: "It is all one, therefore I say: 'He destroys the innocent and the wicked' " [Job 9:22]. Moses said: "It is all one, all are equal before You, one decree for the righteous and the wicked." Solomon too says: "All things come alike to all, there is one event to the righteous and the wicked, to the good and clean and the unclean" [Eccles. 9:2]. "The good" refers to Moses . . . the "clean" to Aaron . . . "the unclean" to the spies [those who praised the land and those who maligned it were equally barred from entering it].

Tanchuma, Va'etchanan 1

MOSES SOUGHT TO LIFT the ban which barred him from crossing the Jordan. Human judges occasionally amend a prior decision upon hearing a plea for reconsideration. The introduction of new facts may lessen the degree of culpability of a defendant, or at least make him worthy of compassion. However, a plea to God to reconsider His judgment is incompatible with our concept of a God who is omniscient and is at all times aware of all the facts and circumstances. Yet Moses pleaded with God to reconsider His decree.

According to the Bible, prayer is effective in obtaining relief from heavenly punishment. Abraham's prayer saved the life of King Avimelech (Gen. 20:7). Moses' prayer brought relief to Miriam (Num. 12:13). King Hezekiah's prayer averted his premature death (II Kings 20:5).

There are two types of decrees, contingent and absolute. The punishment of Avimelech was aimed at obtaining the release of Sarah. When this goal was achieved, the decree lapsed. Miriam's punishment aimed at her reconciliation with Moses. Moses' prayer achieved that end. The punishment of Hezekiah was intended,

101

according to the Talmud, to compel him to abandon his celibacy and provide heirs for the Davidic dynasty (Berachot 10a). That too was achieved shortly after his prayer.

Absolute decrees, on the other hand, are not designed to obtain specific ends. Tradition recognizes that such decrees are irreversible (asarah harugei malchut). On what basis did Moses plead for reconsideration?

Tanchuma offers two explanations: (1) Job charged God with injustice and eventually obtained relief. Moses did likewise. (2) Moses did not charge God with injustice but merely pleaded that there was an appearance of injustice and, like Ecclesiastes, deplored it. Once before, after the golden calf incident, Moses had obtained the removal of God's decree against the Jews because the decree would have had an appearance of injustice in the eyes of the Egyptians (Exod. 32:12, 14). Obviously, Moses' plea was more readily accepted when he pleaded for the Jewish people than when he pleaded for himself.

The Biblical Reward of Long Life

EKKEB

"And it shall come to pass, because you hearken to these commands . . . He will love you and bless you" [Deut. 7:12–13]. Rabbi Simon B. Yochai taught: "God revealed the reward of two commands, one minor and one major. The minor command orders the release of a mother bird from the nest prior to the taking of its young [Deut. 22:7]. Those who comply with this command will be rewarded with long life [ibid.] A similar reward is promised to those who honor their parents" [ibid. 5:16].

Tanchuma, Ekkeb 2

"And God your Lord will keep with you the covenant" [Deut. 7:12]. Whatever Jews are eating in this world is due to Balaam's blessing. The blessings which they received from the patriarchs and the prophets are reserved for the future to come.

Yalkut 848

ACCORDING TO TANCHUMA, the Torah revealed the reward of a minor and a major command to caution people against neglecting minor commands on the assumption that their reward is negligible. There is an indirect allusion in this statement to the anomaly of the righteous who suffer. Some observers of major commands may fall short because they neglect the minor commands.

The Yalkut is more direct in its treatment of this question. The promise of a long life is nearly always bracketed with the phrase "on the earth which the Lord has given you." In most instances the promise is addressed to those who abide by the laws of the Torah and also to their offspring. It is clear that the biblical promise of

103

long life is to be taken as a promise to the nation that it will have a long existence in its own land.

The injunction "A perfect and just weight shall you have" [Deut. 25:15] is another command which promises the reward of long life. The three commands project three conditions essential to national longevity—the traits of honesty and compassion, and a firm foundation of strong family units.

The Yalkut reasserts the traditional belief that God's rewards are reserved for the world-to-come or the messianic era. Jewish existence in the diaspora has regretfully depended upon the whim of the Balaams, the non-Jewish spiritual forces of Christianity and Islam. They set the limits of the Jewish share of worldly goods. Whatever Jews ate was by their sufferance.

The diminished influence of the Balaams of this world makes it possible for a Jewish state to exist despite the hostility of Islam and the refusal of the Vatican to grant this state diplomatic recognition. We must pray that God's promise of a long national Jewish existence will bring about the acceptance of Israel by all the nations of the world.

Transferal of Guilt

"Behold, I set before you this day a blessing and a curse" [Deut. 11:26]. It is written: "Do not evil and good proceed out of the mouth of the Most High?" [Lam. 3:38]. Rabbi Abin said: "When the Jews stood at Mount Sinai, God gave them the Torah. Since then, only those who were guilty of sin have been punished by God. Prior to that time, a whole generation was punished for the transgressions of the sinners in their midst. Thus many people who were just as righteous as Noah perished in the flood."

Tanchuma, Re'eh 3

ACCORDING TO RABBI ABIN, blessings and curses coexist in every generation. The saint and the sinner are judged on their merits, and the former will not suffer for the derelictions of the latter. Moses' offer of a choice between a blessing and a curse was addressed to each Jew individually, not to the nation as a whole. Each individual will either reap the reward or suffer the consequence of his choice.

The old doctrine of collective accountability was terminated, according to Rabbi Abin, at Mount Sinai. It would have been highly inequitable to punish a monotheistic nation for the sins of pagans. However, monotheism was central to the seven Noahide laws. We must therefore assume that the old doctrine of the transferal of guilt was abrogated soon after the flood. Indeed that is the implication of God's declaration: "Neither will I again smite every living thing [the innocent and the guilty], as I have done" (Gen. 8:21).

Abraham was apparently unaware of the abrogation of the old doctrine when he pleaded with God to spare the innocent people of Sodom. God assured him that the righteous, if any, would be spared (ibid. 18:26).

105

It seems that the old doctrine was partially retained within the narrow confines of the family. The iniquity of fathers is visited upon their children unto the fourth generation (Exod. 20:5). The rabbis limited this visitation to children who persist in the ancestral sin (Sanhedrin 27b). Deuteronomy rejects any trace of the old doctrine (24:16), and Ezekiel confirmed the total elimination of transferal of guilt (18:4).

Most religions and modern civil codes do not accept the notion of collective accountability. Yet many people of all creeds and races, however, are still guilty of the sin of generalization. Crimes committed by members of an identifiable group are instantaneously attributed to the entire group. Ezekiel protested against this common reaction. "The righteousness of the righteous shall be upon him, and upon his own self the wickedness of the wicked will come to be" (18:20).

All people must be judged on their merits and not by the label attached to them.

The Essence of Judaism

SHOFETIM

Rabbi Shimelai said: "Six hundred and thirteen commands were given to Moses on Mount Sinai. The essence of these commands was distilled by David [in the Book of Psalms] into eleven . . . Isaiah condensed them into six . . . Micah into three . . . Amos into two . . . Habakkuk into one."

Tanchuma, Shofetim 9

THE TORAH PROVIDES GUIDELINES for human behavior that will lead to perfection. Which of these guidelines are most representative of the spirit of Judaism? Which contribute most to the goal of perfection? The psalmist was the first biblical author to publish his selection: uprightness, righteousness, and sincerity; abstention from slander and evil, and from putting another person to shame; hatred of vile people, honoring God-fearing persons, and upholding the sanctity of oaths; rejection of usury and of bribes (15:1–5).

It is remarkable that most of the commands in the psalmist's list fall within the category of man's relations with his fellowman (*bein adam lachavero*) rather than man's obligations to God (*bein adam lamakom*). It is even more remarkable that the psalmist introduces his list with the following sentence: "Lord, who shall sojourn in your tabernacle, and who shall dwell upon your high mountain?" The privilege of living in God's tabernacle depends in part upon the merit of man's relations with other men.

One who fails to practice honesty (oath), charitableness (usury), and justice (bribes) can never consider himself as being close to God merely because he is a God-fearing individual. The talmudic sage Mar Ukva censures even more severely those who are guilty of unethical conduct: "The Almighty and the arrogant cannot exist in the same world" (Sotah 5a). According to another talmudic quotation: "Slanderers and I [God] cannot exist in the same world" (Arachin 15b).

Isaiah's list has the following selection: righteousness, uprightness, and abstention from oppression, bribery, plots to commit bloodshed, and evil.

Micah declared: "Do justice, love mercy, and walk humbly with God" (6:8). He gave precedence to man's proper treatment of his fellowman over man's commitment to God. The latter comes under the rubric of righteousness, which heads Isaiah's list.

Amos condensed the spirit of Judaism in a succinct phrase: "Seek Me [God] and live" [in harmony with others] (5:4).

Habakkuk proclaimed: "The righteous shall live by his faith" (2:4). Faith is the essence of the entire Torah. One is faithful to God only when one understands that the laws regulating man's behavior in society are just as important as the laws which prescribe man's commitment to God. Habakkuk's choice of an all-embracing faith was echoed by the psalmist: "The fear of the Lord is the beginning of wisdom" (111:10). The Torah is the repository of Jewish wisdom.

The Price of War

"When you go forth in camp against your enemy . . . if there be among you a man that is not clean . . . he shall go out of the camp. . . . And it shall be when evening comes up, he shall bathe himself in the water, and when the sun goes down he may come within the camp" [Deut. 23:10–12]. "The man who is not clean" is an Israelite who was contaminated by idolatry. . . . "Shall go out of the camp" [predicts] the exile to Babylonia. "When evening comes up" [refers to] the evening of Babylonia . . . "Bathe himself in water" [promises] the cleansing of the Jews by God. "When the sun goes down" [alludes] to the coming of the Messiah. "He may come within the camp" [proclaims] the return of the exiles and the restoration of the Temple.

Tanchuma, Ki Tetze 3

THE OPENING VERSE OF Ki Tetze warns of the incidence of inter-marriage when young Jewish soldiers are separated from their families in time of war and encounter non-Jewish females (Deut. 21:10–11). This is followed by laws pertaining to marital strife (ibid. 21:15) and a "rebellious son" (ibid. 21:18). These too, according to the rabbis, result from the disruption of normal conditions in the aftermath of war (Tanchuma, Ki tetze 1).

Wartime tensions foster an atmosphere of permissiveness. Rape and other sexual offenses, discussed in the next biblical chapter, are further symptoms of the moral breakdown of a society under the pressure of war (ibid. 22:13–29).

The phrase *ki tetze*, connoting going out on a military expedition, is repeated twice in this portion. The first one (Deut. 21:10) is addressed to each individual soldier to caution him against the pitfalls of war. The second, (Deut. 23:10) is addressed to the *macha-*

neh, the collective encampment of men, to warn them of potential transgressions which may affect the national character. The Midrash reads into this passage a forecast of a crucial period in Jewish history. The "uncleanliness" is idolatry, a national offense which lingered on until the end of the Judean kingdom. The Jews will have to "go out" into exile to Babylonia, where they will be cleansed from the sin of idolatry. Salvation will come in the "evening" of the Babylonian kingdom, when it will be conquered by King Cyrus. The Messiah will make it possible for the exiles to go back "within the camp" (Judea and the Temple).

The midrashic reference to the Messiah is obviously an allusion to Cyrus, whom Isaiah called God's anointed (*meshicho*, 45:1).

The Bible does not outlaw wars. However, by stressing the great cost of war, in terms of the attrition of spiritual and ethical values, it strongly discourages military engagements unless there is no alternative.

The Blind Man Who Gropes in the Dark

KI TAVO

We have learned: Rabbi Jose said: "All my life I have been dis-turbed by [my incomprehension of] the following verse: 'And you shall grope at noonday, as the blind gropes in darkness' [Deut. 28:29]. Does it matter to the blind whether it is dark or light? Until an experience provided an answer. It was late at night when I saw a blind man walking with a torch in his hand. [I asked him:] 'of what use is the torch to you?' He replied: 'When the torch is in my hand, people see me and keep me from falling into pits.' "

Yalkut, Ki Tavo 939

MOSES WARNED THE JEWS of the heavenly punishment in store for those who violate the Torah. He presented the image of a blind man groping in the dark, who suffers doubly from being helpless and from having no one to help him.

Indeed, the tragic plight of the Jewish people throughout the Dark Ages was not unlike the plight of the biblical blind man. They were subjected to cruel oppression and not a single voice of sympathy was ever raised in their defense. They suffered in darkness, alone and unseen.

When the iron shutters, which kept the light out of the sordid Jewish ghettos, were pried ajar, permitting some gray light to filter in, the Dark Ages came to an end. The world was at last able to catch a glimpse of a tottering "blind man." The hideous scene rattled the conscience of some decent people. England was the first Christian nation to protest to a foreign leader, the Empress Maria Theresa of Austria, when she decreed, in 1748, that the Jews of Bohemia were to be expelled.

It was not until the Holocaust that the full glare of the world's

111

spotlight revealed the indescribable tragedy of Jewish martyrdom. The shock evoked a flood of sympathy, and the end result was the creation of the State of Israel.

Regretfully, the evil that possesses the minds of some men must never be underestimated. A "revisionist" school of history has emerged and set as its goal the denial of the Holocaust. Its true aim is the extinction of the spotlight, to the end that Jews may once again suffer in the dark.

The imagery of Moses ' "blind man," who faces his troubled life unseen, has colored Jewish relations with the world at large and has also affected the ability of Jews to cope with the internal problem of assimilation. This corrosive process, nearly unseen and unnoticed, has accelerated at an alarming pace. While modern Jewry lavishes its resources on social action and self-defense, some of the finest of its youth are slipping away in the dark. Assimilation is a serious problem, worsened by apparent ignorance of its existence.

Jewish National Resurrection

NITZAVIM

"You are standing this day" [Deut. 29:9]. [Fallen nations never rise to stand again]. Israel falls but rises to stand once more.

Yalkut, Nitzavim 940

MOSES ADDRESSED THIS STERN admonition, warning against the betrayal of God, to the heads, tribes, elders, officers, and all of Israel (Deut. 29:9). He also took note of the presence of children, wives, and strangers who had joined the Jewish camp. His unique salutation reflects an intensive effort to get everyone within hearing range to grasp the momentous significance of the occasion, the induction of the Jewish people into nationhood.

"You are standing here today," Moses' voice rang out, that He [God] may establish you . . . unto Himself for a nation" (ibid. 29:12). To emphasize the national aspect of the induction, he listed all the various ranks and groups essential to national existence.

The author of the Midrash, who stressed Jewish resilience, lived in the postexilic period, when Jews no longer enjoyed national status. The history of all extinct ancient empires gave little reason for anticipating a Jewish national resurrection. Yet the midrashic author was not impressed by the past experience of other nations.

Moses had warned the Jewish people of the dire disasters that might befall them in the future if they failed to abide by God's commands. Yet he assured them that Jews would never disappear off the face of the earth. Eventually, when they repented and returned to God, they would be restored to their land (ibid. 30:1–10). To emphasize the permanence of the Jewish people, Moses used the verb *nitzavim* ("stand") in place of the commonly used *omedim*, because of the former's connotation of a firm position, of permanence.

113

There was a universal non-Jewish conviction, prior to the establishment of Israel, that Jews could never regain national status. This conclusion, based on ancient history, was forcefully expressed by Henry Wadsworth Longfellow in "The Jewish Cemetery at Newport": "Dead nations never rise again."

Why did the Jews turn out to be an exception to the general rule? Religious Zionists find the answer in the portion of Nitzavim. The establishment of Israel is an implementation of God's promise: "The Lord your God will bring you into the land which your fathers possessed, and you will possess it" (ibid. 30:5).

One must not overlook the psychological factor, which accounts for the distinction in reactions to national defeat. The peoples of the ancient empires gave up all hope of national resurrection and soon lost their specific identity. Jews, on the other hand, were inspired by the Bible never to give up hope of redemption. The eventual redemption of the hope was thus made possible.

The Hard of Hearing

"When all Israel is come to appear before the Lord your God, you shall read the Torah before all Israel in their ears [be'ozneihem]. Assemble [hakhel] the people . . . that they may hear, that they may learn to observe" [Deut. 31:11–12]. Rabbi Tanchuma said: "A person who is deaf in one ear is exempt from making an appearance [because the Torah cannot be read in both ears].

Chagigah

RABBI TANCHUMA'S OPINION that the phrase "in their ears" (plural) excludes people who have hearing in only one ear is borne out by the explanation stated in the next verse: "that they may hear" (*yishme'u*). Perfect hearing is of the essence to the achievement of the goal of the mitzvah of *hakhel*, the teaching of Torah. Hence the need for hearing in both ears.

Admittedly, the verb *shamoa* has a variety of other nuances in addition to hearing. It could mean to pay attention, to heed, to learn, to observe, to comprehend. However, these functions would not be advanced by "reading in their ears" as would the function of hearing.

There are other mitzvot which call for hearing. The benediction preceding the blowing of the shofar on Rosh Hashanah defines the mitzvah as an injunction to hear the sound of the shofar. Yet there is no qualifying phrase in the text which demands that the sound of the shofar reach both ears. That is the reason why impaired hearing does not exempt one from this mitzvah. Why was *hakhel* an exception to this rule?

From a midrashic point of view, the mitzvah of *hakhel* lays down guidelines to be applied on all occasions which aim to achieve the goal of *hakhel*, the spread of religious education. Should the on-

115

going communal obligation to promote educational projects be directed at all individuals who are ignorant of their Jewish traditions? Are there any exemptions?

There are some who are totally ignorant of the Torah but are willing to hear and to learn. No effort should be spared in providing them with an education. Such is the case with a high percentage of the Russian emigres and with some young people born into assimilated Jewish families.

There are people who have a garbled knowledge of Jewish traditions and labor under many misconceptions which generate negative attitudes. No amount of instruction and information will make a dent in their resistance to opposing views. They may appear to give a polite hearing to all voices. In reality, they turn a deaf ear. The information is passed into one ear and out the other. Rabbi Tanchuma feels that the community is exempt from spending its resources on such individuals. If they do not have perfect hearing, the community should turn its attention to those who do.

Rain and Dew

HA'AZINU

"My message shall drop as the rain, my speech shall proceed as the dew" [Deut. 32:2]. Rav Judah said: "The day when it rains is as important as the day when the Torah was given." Rava said: "The day when it rains is more important than the day when the Torah was given."

Yalkut, Ha'azinu 942

MOSES PRAYED THAT HIS WORDS would nurture the Jewish soul like the rain which nourishes the Jewish soil. His use of the similes of rain and dew is in need of an interpretation of their symbolic implications. The rain drops fall from above to breathe life into the earth. Dew, on the other hand, rises from below to moisten the growing vegetation. Nature thus provides a model for man to follow.

The religious consciousness of most people is nourished by instruction provided from above by parents, teachers, and enlightened leaders. However, the educational guidance offered from above is most effective when it interacts with a quest of knowledge, which like dew rises from below.

The rapid assimilation of modern Jews, living in a climate of freedom, is not the result of a shortage of instruction given from above. It is rather due to the absence of a search for knowledge rising from below. The recent emergence of a receptive mood on the part of some of our youth is responsible for the phenomenon of the *baalei teshuvah*.

Rain has an additional symbolic significance. It consists of gentle small drops which combine to enrich the soil. However, the raging fury of torrential rains, when the water drenches the earth in overflowing outbursts, results in devastation and destruction. Such is the threat posed by the fundamentalist religious movements which have inundated many lands.

117

Rav Judah and Rava gave an insightful dimension to the simile of rain. Moses had written the Torah and turned over the inscribed testament to the Jewish people (Deut. 31:9) with a simultaneous command that it be read publicly at the *hakhel* assembly. On the same day he also delivered Ha'azinu (Deut. 31:22). By invoking the simile of rain, he drew a comparison between the memorable day on which he had given the Torah to the Jews and the day on which the rain falls.

Moses had previously informed the people that observance of the commands of the Torah would bring God's reward of rain (ibid. 11:14). On the other hand, the punishment for disobedience would be the withholding of rain (ibid. 17). Rav Judah said that the day of rain, which testifies to obedience to the Torah, is as important as the day when the Torah was given to them. Rava said it is even more important. Of what use is the Torah if the people do not observe its commands?

Conditional Blessings

VEZOT HABERACHAH

"And this is the blessing" [Deut. 33:1]. It was the practice of the prophets to begin [their discourses] with harsh words and end with words of comfort.

Yalkut, Vezot Haberachah 949

"Many daughters have done valiantly" [Prov. 31:29] alludes to the blessings of Moses. The Patriarchs blessed their children [unconditionally], but they suffered from [sibling] strife.

Tanchuma, Vezot Haberachah 1

THE TEXT OF ABRAHAM'S BLESSING is not recorded in the Torah. We assume that it was modeled after the angel's blessing following the *akeidah*. It was probably paraphrased as follows: "May your seed multiply as the stars of heaven and the sand which is upon the seashore. May your seed possess the gate of his enemies" (Gen. 22:17). This blessing was not linked to any warning of a forfeiture of God's favor in the event of the seed's abandonment of the faith.

Isaac's blessing, initially intended for Esau but conferred upon Jacob (ibid. 27:28–29, 33) was similarly given with no strings attached.

Jacob followed the same pattern in his blessings of Ephraim and Manasseh (ibid. 48:16) and most of his sons (ibid. 49:8–27).

Moses, on the other hand, opened his remarks with a warning of the dire consequences of misconduct: "But it shall come to pass, if you do not hearken unto the voice of the Lord . . . that all these curses shall come upon you" (Deut. 28:15). Having thus cautioned the Jewish people, he concluded his long discourse with Vezot Haberachah.

The flawed sibling relationships of the Patriarchs' children stands out in contrast to the smooth and harmonious relationship between the tribes of Israel during the critical years of the conquest of Canaan. The warriors of the tribes in that period were the very men who had listened to Moses' warnings and promises, his curses and blessings. The Midrash properly concluded that a conditional blessing is an effective deterrent against questionable behavior.

The relevance of the midrashic conclusion extends to many situations which affect political and social relations. The conflict with Iraq in 1991 was in a great measure due to the massive weaponry lavished upon its rogue government by the aggrieved nations, with no restrictions attached. Parents who shower money on their spoiled children, with no corrective aim, do not act out of love.

The Midrash (Yalkut 951) notes that Moses was called an *ish mitzri* at the outset of his career (Exod. 2:19). He was thus identified by Jethro's daughters because he repelled the attacking shepherds. To act out of compassion is a human instinct. At the end of his career, Moses was called *ish hoElokim* (Deut. 33:1). He earned that title because he restrained his compassion for the ultimate good of his people. That was a demonstration of true love.

Jethro's daughters blessed Moses, that was noble. However, Moses' blessing of Israel was the most noble of all.

FESTIVALS

Occupation and Preoccupation

ROSH HASHANAH

*"In the seventh month, in the first day of the month, shall . . . be a
memorial proclaimed with the blast of a horn" [Lev. 23:24]. Rabbi
Abba said: "All year long Jews are busy with their work. On Rosh
Hashanah they take their shoferot and blow before the Almighty
. . . and [He] is filled with compassion for them."*

Vayikra Rabbah 29

A PLEA FOR MERCY GENERALLY amounts to an admission of guilt.
However, in the event of a miscarriage of justice, a plea for mercy
merely reasserts a claim of innocence. Thus Jacob's prayer that
"God give you [his sons] mercy before the man [Joseph]" (Gen. 43:14)
conceded no guilt because he was convinced of his sons' innocence.

There is no miscarriage of justice in the heavenly tribunal, and
one cannot contend that heaven's judgment is erroneous. A plea for
mercy is therefore a petition for a pardon, despite the admitted
guilt. On the other hand, when mercy is not invoked, one may assert
his innocence and pray that God will vindicate him. This is the
sense of the eleventh benediction: "Reign over us, O Lord, in kind-
ness and mercy, and clear us in judgment." If we are guilty, we plead
for mercy. If not, proclaim our innocence.

The ancient Jews, according to the Midrash, were in need of
mercy on Rosh Hashanah, and they evoked it by blowing the shofar.
What were they guilty of? They were guilty of being *oskim bimelachtom*, busy with their tasks all year long. Is that sinful?

Oskim bimelachtom, in contrast to *osim et melachtom* ("do their
work"), has an ambivalent connotation. It may mean "occupied" or
"preoccupied" with work, to the exclusion of all else. The exclusivist
rendition is implied in the rabbinic dictum: *ha'osek bemitzvah
patur min hamitzvah* ("one who is preoccupied with a mitzvah is
exempt from performing other mitzvot," Sukkah 25a).

123

Ancient Jewish farmers were totally absorbed by their multiple chores and had little time left for other tasks. It was not until Rosh Hashanah that their blasts on the shofar signaled the end of their preoccupation with the land and the diversion of their attention to their relation with God. God's mercy was thus evoked.

The sweatshop Jew at the turn of this century was not unlike the ancient Jewish farmer. So are many modern Jews who pursue the elusive goal of success. Hopefully, the blast of the shofar will remind them that there are many other goals, domestic and national, which await their attention. If not now, when?

Jeremiah's Warning to the Nations of the World

ROSH HASHANAH

"In the seventh month" [Lev. 23:24]. [It is written:] "For I will bring to a full end [chalah] all the nations where I have driven you" [Jer. 46:28]. The nations who reap their fields to the very end [mechalin] [and leave nothing for the poor and the stranger] will I bring to an end. [On the other hand,] "you [Jews] I will not bring to an end" (ibid.) because Israel does not reap the fields to their end, in keeping with the injunction in a prior verse: "You shall not wholly reap [lo sechale] the corner of the field" [the law of pe'ah].*

Vayikra Rabbah 29

THE MIDRASH POINTS TO A link between the law of *pe'ah* and Rosh Hashanah (ibid. 23:24). On that traditional day of judgment, man's record of religious observance is examined. The entire range of the Judaic fabric is scrutinized. It is rather strange that the Midrash selected a single law, the law of *pe'ah*, as the sole mitzvah upon which God's judgment hinges.

The midrashic reference to the law of *pe'ah* can only be understood when placed within the context of Jeremiah's prophecy. Jeremiah addressed his remarks to the scattered remnants of Israel, fearful of the cruelty of some of the host nations. He reassured them: "Fear not, O Jacob, for I am with you; for I will bring a full end to the nations where I have driven you."

God will condemn the nations who reap their fields to the end, showing no consideration for their own poor people and not welcoming the stranger. Such nations will be brought to extinction.

By linking the law of *pe'ah* to Rosh Hashanah the Midrash indicates that Rosh Hashanah transcends its parochial role as a Jewish day of judgment. The selfish nations of the world, whose vile deeds have bloodied the Jewish people and have ground their own citizens into the dust, will also be judged on Rosh Hashanah. Unlike the Jews, who stand individually before God on that day, the non-Jews stand collectively before God to justify their national existence.

The concept of a universal day of judgment is stated in the brief prayer of *Hayom harat olam*. This phrase has its origin in Jeremiah (20:17). It means "an everlasting conception." The world and all its living creatures were left by God in a sheltered global womb to grow, develop, and mature. All nations must prove that they are part of a process which leads to progress and perfection. If not, they are in danger of ending their existence in a stillborn death.

Good Intentions and Evil Consequences

YOM KIPPUR

Rabbi Eliezer said: "It is written: 'From all your sins shall you be clean before the Lord' [Lev. 16:30]. Yom Kippur atones for actions of whose sinfulness only God is aware."

Keritut 25b

THE PRAYER *AL CHET* lists a category of sins which are committed unwittingly by some people (*belo yodim*) due to absentmindedness or ignorance of the law. Despite the lack of penitence on the part of the transgressor, divine forgiveness may properly be expected.

Rabbi Eliezer points to an additional category of sins. The act is not sinful per se, and the intent behind it is praiseworthy, but under some circumstances the act may have a potential for harmful consequences, and due to human misjudgment some people fail to perceive it.

If a person advocates a policy in the belief that it will lead to positive results, he will express no regrets until events show him to have been wrong. Yet in the eyes of God the supposed good deed may be a grievous sin. Rabbi Eliezer magnanimously interprets the phrase "before the Lord" (Lev. 16:30) as a promise that such sins will be forgiven.

Rabbi Eliezer's category of sins is more common than is generally realized. Some parents pressure their children to attain desirable careers. Regretfully, they ignore or misjudge the limitations of their children's potential. In such cases parental intentions look good but may lead to disastrous results.

A soft-hearted individual who refuses to press charges against a criminal is guilty of a compassion which leads to the proliferation of crime and the victimization of innocent people.

The impulse to protect the homeless and to ease their miserable lot is surely noble. To insist that they have a vested right to assemble in public places, even when they pose a danger to the general community, is to ignore the safety of the many who have not contributed to the misery of the few.

To promote and defend the civil rights of all people is highly commendable. To fight for the right of bigots to march provocatively in the areas of their intended targets is a miscarriage of justice.

To exalt and preach peace is most admirable. Those who pressure Israel to agree to the establishment of an independent, but not viable, Palestinian state are guilty of self-delusion and a failure to perceive that such a step would be a prelude to bloodshed and self-destruction.

We assume that Yom Kippur atones only when the good intentions are dropped in time before they produce the evil consequences.

The Merit of Prayer and Penitence

YOM KIPPUR

"Take Aaron and his sons with him" [Lev. 8:2]. [Why was Aaron's involvement in the worship of the golden calf forgiven?] Rabbi Judah said: "Penitence averts half [of the punishment]. Prayer averts all of it." Rabbi Joshua bar Levi said: "Penitence averts all, prayer averts half."

Vayikra Rabbah 10

AARON'S CONSECRATION SIGNALED his total exoneration from sin. Was it prayer or penitence which led to his vindication? Rabbi Judah attributed it to prayer, and Rabbi Joshua bar Levi to penitence.

Aaron's apologetical explanation to Moses included neither a prayer nor an expression of regret (Exod. 32:22). He pleaded duress in his defense. In view of the rabbinic consensus that duress does not excuse the sin of idolatry, both rabbis assumed that Aaron was indeed penitent and had prayed for forgiveness. They differed, however, as to whether the prayer or the penitence contributed most to God's forgiveness.

When God expressed His intent to destroy the Jewish people in the aftermath of the golden calf, it was Moses' prayer which won divine forgiveness (ibid. 14). Since he was personally blameless he could not appear in the role of a penitent.

The analysis of the relative merits of prayer and penitence is not recorded in the Midrash. This leaves us free to interpret the rabbis' opposing views. Rabbi Judah attributed greater effectiveness to prayer because of the tradition that God is fond of the prayers of the righteous, and one may add, of those who strive to become righteous. It is taken for granted that such prayers reflect a truly peniten-

129

tial mood. Penitence, without prayer, is not to be taken as a plea to be spared from punishment. Many a penitent welcomes retribution as a means of paying his debt to God and man.

Rabbi Joshua bar Levi probably felt that prayers are self-serving. Only full penitence can elicit complete forgiveness.

Regardless of the relative merits of prayer and penitence, a combination of both is essential if one is to deserve forgiveness. This is true of wrongs committed by individuals and also of those committed by nations on a national scale.

Recent upheavals in Eastern Europe brought an end to tyrannical regimes that had supported international terrorism. Most admitted their dreary record, but only one nation begged for forgiveness and expressed its deep regrets. Are we to be more godly than God and extend forgiveness even in the absence of prayer and penitence?

The Lulav and the Hyssop

SUKKOT

"You shall take on the first day the fruit of a goodly tree" [Lev. 23:40]. Rabbi Abba Bar Kahana said: "From the reward for the 'taking' [of the hyssop in Egypt]. [Exod. 12:22] we can learn the reward for the 'taking' [of a lulav]."

Vayikra Rabbah, Emor 30

Rabbi Judah said: "A bound [lulav] is kosher. If it is loose, it may not be used." He came to this conclusion by comparing the "taking" [of the lulav] *to the "taking" [of the hyssop]. Just as the one [hyssop] was made up of a bunch [agudat eizov]. So the other [lulav] has to be bunched together.*

Yalkut 651

SUKKOT AND PASSOVER HAVE BEEN linked in rabbinic homiletic and halachic literature. The link between them is explicitly established in a biblical text: "You shall dwell in booths [because] I made the children of Israel to dwell in booths, when I took them out of Egypt" (Lev. 23:43). "Hence we learn that Sukkot, too, commemorates the exodus from Egypt" (Sifra, Emor 207). The first location reached by the Israelites after their departure from Rameses was Sukkot (Exod. 12:37). The report of this leg of their journey supplements the chronicle of the exodus.

The biblical linking of the two major festivals is based on their identical commemoration of the exodus. The rabbis extended this link by associating the "taking" of the *lulav* with the "taking" of the hyssop.

The hyssop was used for the sprinkling of blood in two sacrificial rites—the cleansing of impurity and contamination (Num. 19:18) and the recovery from leprosy (Lev. 14:7). In other rites where sprinkling of blood was required, the priest used his finger to sprinkle small quantities of blood (Lev. 4:6, 17, 30; 9:9).

A brush made of hyssop scooped up much blood and left a large visible stain of blood on the area where the brush was applied. When it was desirable to publicize a specific rite, the hyssop brush was used because of the prominence of its stroke. This was essential to inform the people that normal contacts might be resumed with an individual who had previously been unclean or a leper. The isolation of the unclean or the leper was at an end. In private rites, in which the public at large had no interest, the sprinkling was symbolic and the priest used his finger to sprinkle some drops of blood.

The hyssop in Egypt publicized the intervention by God that made the impending exodus possible without any interference by the Egyptians. The *lulav*, too, celebrated the bounty of the land and publicized God's intervention and protection, which in this instance made Jewish independence possible, without any interference by hostile nations.

A Commemoration of the Exodus

SUKKOT

"You shall dwell in booths [because] I made the children of Israel to dwell in booths when I took them out of Egypt" [Lev. 23:42–43]. Hence we learn that Sukkot also commemorates the Exodus.

Sifra, Emor 207

GOD PROVIDED BOOTHS FOR THE children of Israel upon their arrival at Sukkot on the fifteenth of Nissan (Yalkut 208). Why is this event commemorated on the fifteenth of Tishri? The Sifra merely points to the exodus symbolism of the *sukkah* without commenting on the relevance of the date of Sukkot to the supplying of booths on Passover.

The account of the exodus, central to the development of Judaism, is a pervasive theme which is stressed throughout the year in our daily, Sabbath, and festival prayers. The impact of the exodus would be diminished if the recitation of the story did not include a mention of the oppression which preceded it. "From Egypt you redeemed us . . . from bondage you delivered us."

The Torah texts which prescribe the commemoration of the exodus give little emphasis to the prior tyranny (Exod. 12:17; 13:3, 8–9, 14; Deut. 16:3). The injunction to eat bitter herbs made sure that the slavery was not overlooked completely in the midst of the celebration of freedom.

There were two occasions when the Egyptian slavery was given great publicity, in the celebration of the festival of Shavuot (ibid. 16:12) and in the recitation associated with the offering of *bikkurim* (ibid. 26:6–7). On both occasions the text stresses the need for sharing one's bounty with the underprivileged. A recollection of the poverty and suffering in Egypt will inspire greater responsiveness to

133

the needs of the deprived. Of the two momentous events on the fifteenth of Nissan, the matzot and the booths, only the former was designated as a reminder of the "day" of the exodus (Exod. 12:17, 13:3). Matzot must therefore be eaten on the anniversary of the exodus.

There are other rituals which commemorate the redemption of Passover, but not the "day" of the redemption. These may be observed at other times of the year. Such are the mitzvah of tefillin (ibid. 13:9), the law of the redemption of the firstborn (ibid. 15), the dwelling in booths (Lev. 23:43), and bikkurim (ibid. 26:8).

Sukkot was the only pilgrimage festival which celebrated the harvest. Unlike Shavuot, it was not linked to Passover and it has no ritual commemorating the exodus. That need was filled by the sukkah, a vivid reminder of the booths which God had provided on the day of the exodus. Jews were ordered to dwell in booths without dwelling upon the period of slavery and affliction which preceded the exodus from Egypt.

A Rabbinic Definition of Heroism

CHANUKAH

"[We Thank You] for the miracles . . . and the wars which You waged . . . in the days of Mattathias . . . the hasmonean . . . when the wicked Greek kingdom rose . . . to make them forget your Torah. . . . You avenged their wrongs . . . for Yourself You made a great and holy name in your world."

Chanukah Prayer, Al HaNisim

THE PRAYER STRIKINGLY OMITS any praise of the Hasmoneans' martial skills and their contribution to the victory. The name of Mattathias is mentioned merely as a time reference. This parallels the Passover Haggadah, which omits the name of Moses and attributes the victory solely to the direct intervention of God.

Biblical texts give military heroes laudatory recognition. The wars of Moses, Joshua, the judges, and the kings were carefully noted and recorded. Samson became a popular hero despite his lack of moral stature. Saul and David were eulogized in folk ballads. The acquisition of military skill and experience was strongly advocated in the Book of Judges (3:2).

In contrast to biblical practice, rabbinic leaders discouraged the adulation of postbiblical military figures. The Hasmoneans who belonged to the "priestly tribe" the Kohanim forfeited rabbinic support when they assumed royal rank in disregard of the talmudic doctrine that "priests are not eligible for royal anointment." This doctrine was based on the conviction that temporal power would corrupt the priesthood.

The Talmud has no praise for the last-ditch defenders of Jerusalem who fought to the bitter end against the legions of Rome even when defeat was imminent and inevitable. The heroic last stand of

135

the defenders of Masada was not eulogized in the pages of the Talmud. The doomed rebellion of Bar Kochba, at the cost of countless thousands of young Jewish men, did not win the admiration of contemporary rabbinic leaders. They obviously condemned bloodshed in struggles foredoomed to failure. However, they greatly admired the heroic perseverance of the people, who refused to give up their devotion to the faith and their bright hopes, even in the face of defeat. The triumphant note of the Chanukah prayer is expressed in its concluding sentence: "Thereupon your children came . . . kindled lights in your holy courts."

A nineteenth-century French writer caught the mood of the rabbinic mind in his comment on ancient Jewish military prowess: "The long passive defense . . . is what I admire most in the history of the last day of the Jewish national state. I see in it something more glorious than dying in battle. . . . To have before them an example of a whole world yielding [in defeat] and yet themselves not yielding, is the acme of national heroism." In the mind of this writer, Rabban Yochanan b. Zakkai, who founded the yeshiva at Yavne after Tisha B'av, was a greater national hero than Mattathias the Hasmonean.

Four Stages of Redemption

PURIM

Rabbi Chiyah the Elder and Rabbi Simon Bar Chalafta watched the light of dawn penetrate [the darkness]. . . . Rabbi Chiyah the Elder said: "This is like the redemption of Israel. At first it proceeds a little at a time. As it progresses its pace increases. Thus at the outset 'Mordecai sat at the king's gate' [Esther 2:21]. Then 'Haman took the apparel and the horse' [ibid. 6:11]. After that 'Mordecai returned to the king's gate' [ibid. 6:12]. Finally, 'The Jews had light and gladness' " [ibid. 8:16].

Jer. Berachot 1:1

HATE AND GREED HAVE COMMONLY motivated all Hamans and Hitlers. God's response to their wickedness has taken a variety of forms, sometimes direct and perceptible, other times indirect and concealed.

The liberation from Egyptian slavery was the result of God's direct intervention. After two centuries of enslavement, the Israelites were incapable of mounting a campaign of emancipation on their own. When Moses appeared on the scene, the Hebrew slaves were more or less resigned to their fate. On the other hand, the Persian Jews of Mordecai's generation had for a long time enjoyed freedom and equality. They were physically and emotionally capable of resisting oppression. God arranged the circumstances which Mordecai and Esther exploited to rescue the Jews from calamity.

We have witnessed two similar redemptions in our time. The United Nations voted the establishment of Israel, but it took Jewish fighting to make it a reality. On the other hand, the remarkable exodus of Soviet Jews resulted from events over which Jews had no control or input.

Jewish tradition looks to the messianic era to usher in a period of

137

lasting peace which will bring to an end the Purim cycle of Jewish history. Will that period culminate a long process of evolutionary progress, or will it come unexpectedly, initiating a sudden change in human affairs? Rabbi Chiyah the Elder watched the gradual increase in the brightness of the light of dawn and saw in it a premonition of the gradual arrival of the messianic era.

In Rabbi Chiyah's opinion the final redemption will follow several preliminary stages of progress. Some of them may be obscured by our failure to recognize them as essential links to ultimate salvation. Thus Mordecai's first appearance at the king's gate was hardly an auspicious occasion. He was driven there by a deep concern for Esther's welfare. Yet that was the time when he overheard the plotters' dialogue.

We note that the Persian Jews suffered a serious setback after the first preliminary stage of redemption. Yet the redemptive process never came to an end. The interval between the first and second stages was long and painful. The succeeding stages came at shorter intervals.

Should someone ask when the messianic era will begin, Rabbi Chiyah would answer: It may have begun already.

A Reassessment of the Biblical Pharaoh

PASSOVER

"Now there arose a new king over Egypt" [Exod. 1:8]. He was not a new king. Only his decrees were new.

Tanchuma, Shemot 5

WHAT MOTIVATED THIS RABBINIC interpretation, which is incompatible with the biblical text? The answer may lie in a clarification of some of the obscurities in the account of the exodus. The first intimation of a forthcoming period of enslavement was revealed by God to Abraham: ". . . your seed shall be a stranger in a land that is not theirs . . . and they shall afflict them" (Gen. 15:13). Abraham did not ask the reason for such punishment, nor did he voice a protest, as he did for the people of Sodom (ibid. 18:25).

Jacob's reluctance to go to Egypt is also puzzling. He left only after God had told him: "Fear not to go down into Egypt, for I will make you there a great nation" (ibid. 46:3). What was Jacob afraid of?

Prior to his death, Jacob asked Joseph to bury him in the ancestral grave. Joseph promised, but Jacob insisted that Joseph take an oath (ibid. 37:31). Did Jacob suspect that Joseph would not keep his promise?

To resolve these questions, one must grasp the difficulties attending the transition of Jacob's clan into nationhood. In its embryonic stage, the Hebrew national fetus needed ample space for expansion, sufficient time to develop its religious identity and national consciousness. It also needed the womb of a host nation for physical protection. And it had to be isolated to prevent its assimilation into the host nation.

No host nation would normally tolerate the presence of a thriving minority which maintained distinct national aspirations. The host would either expel the undigested group or enslave them in order to protect its own national interests. When God told Abraham that his seed would become a large nation, he understood that enslavement might be the price that his offspring would have to pay for the privilege of their transition into nationhood. A protest would not have been warranted.

The influential position of Joseph made Egypt an ideal host nation. However, Jacob suspected that Pharaoh might not agree to grant the Jews asylum for the period of their transition to nationhood. He might be offering a one-way admission policy to secure their integration and would not permit them to return to Canaan. Jacob turned out to be right. That is the reason why he did not go home after the end of the famine and why the brothers, who feared Joseph, did not return after the death of their father. Joseph was given leave to go and bury his father only because he had taken an oath (ibid. 50:6).

The Midrash points out that the enslavement was not initiated by a new Pharaoh. It was instituted by the same Pharaoh when he realized that the Jews were resisting assimilation.

The Four Cups of Wine

Why do we drink four cups of wine? Rabbi Yochanan . . . said: "To match the four [biblical] expressions of redemption" [Exod. 6:6–7]. Rabbi Joshua B. Levi said: "To match the four cups mentioned in the account of Pharaoh's butler" [Gen. 40:11, 13].

Jer. Pesachim 10:1

RABBI YOCHANAN'S EXPLANATION has been widely accepted, while Rabbi Joshua's opinion is rarely mentioned by rabbinic commentators. Indeed, it is hard to perceive the relevance of the butler's cup to the theme of Passover.

The account of the butler's experience ends with the statement: ". . . yet the butler did not remember Joseph, but forgot him" (Gen. 40:23). The following are some causes of forgetfulness: a physiological deficiency, a self-induced state of mind to escape the memory of a traumatic experience, a subconscious desire to renege on a promise which was reluctantly made in the first place. The internal conflict hastens the process of forgetfulness.

The butler had reason to be grateful to Joseph. Normally, he should have welcomed the opportunity to help his benefactor. However, his memories of the encounter with Joseph were not all that pleasant. He, a high official of the royal court, had to solicit the help of a lowly criminal. What made the encounter even more distasteful was the fact that his benefactor was a Hebrew lad. This must have irked the butler no end, because Joseph's ethnicity stood out in his mind when he reported the incident to Pharaoh after the recovering his memory (Gen. 41:12). All Egyptians treated Semites with disdain. The butler's forgetfulness was real but self-induced.

The Haggadah stresses the mitzvah of relating the story of the exodus. No detail must be forgotten or left out, neither our shameful

141

period of idolatry nor the degrading conditions of slavery. The dark side of our history is to be used as a backdrop for the exhilaration of freedom. To counter the butler's cups of forgetfulness, we drink the cups of remembrance. The enslaved Jews thought that God had forgotten them: we drink a cup to God because He remembered them. Our ancestors vowed at Mount Sinai to commit themselves to the faith: we drink a cup of remembrance that this vow shall not be forgotten.

The portion of B'shalach, in which the story of the exodus is related, ends with an injunction to erase the memory of Amalek. Compromising with evil is a form of slavery. This admonition was forgotten (I Sam. 6:20). When we drink the four cups of wine we pledge to remember the Egyptian slavery and the Holocaust. The exodus and the State of Israel. We also pledge to remember our commitments to God and to our fellowmen.

God's Commitment to the Soil of Israel

SHAVUOT

"Then she arose with her daughters in-law that she might return from the field of Moab" [Ruth 1:6]. To quote one verse: "For the Lord will not abandon His people, neither will He forsake his inheritance [the land]" [Ps. 94:14]. To quote another verse: "For the Lord will not abandon His people for the sake of His great name" [I Sam. 12:22]. . . . The rabbis said: "[God does not abandon] the Jews of Eretz Yisrael, for their own sake and also for the sake of His inheritance. He does not abandon the Jews of other countries, for the sake of His great name."

Ruth Rabbah 1:6

ELIMELECH'S DEPARTURE FROM Bethlehem due to a famine followed a precedent set by Abraham and Jacob (Gen. 12:10, 46:6). The departure of the Patriarchs was never criticized by the rabbis. Elimelech, however, came under severe criticism because of his abandonment of an existing community struggling for survival (Ruth Rabbah 1:1).

Elimelech's luck ran out in Moab. He exhausted his resources and died a poor man. After his death his two sons married Moabite girls and ten years later joined their father in death. The bleak outlook of Elimelech's widow, Naomi, was suddenly brightened by a cheerful report: "The Lord has remembered His people by giving them bread" (Ruth 1:6).

Did God remember only the Jews of Eretz Yisrael, ignoring all other Jews?

The sweeping promise that "God will not forsake His people" is mentioned twice in the Bible. It is addressed to all Jews, regardless

143

of their place of habitation. Yet the motivation of God's support is different with regard to the Jews of Eretz Yisrael.

All Jews are entitled to God's protection if they merit it. In the absence of merit, God may spare the Jewish people if His intervention will contribute to the glorification of His name among the nations of the world. However, there is an additional reason why God protects the Jews of Eretz Yisrael even when they do not fully deserve it. The additional reason is spelled out in the Book of Psalms: "neither will He forsake his inheritance."

In the very first covenant between God and Abraham, God announced His gift of the land of Canaan to Abraham and his offspring (Gen. 15:18). It was a unilateral act which exacted no quid pro quo from Abraham. In effect, God made a commitment to the soil of Eretz Yisrael that it would be possessed by the Jewish people. Jews at times had to be protected to prevent a breach of God's promise to the soil.

There were two Shavuot rituals—the offering of the first fruits of the land, and the offering of a new-meal (minchah chadashah; Exod. 23:19, Lev. 23:16). Both rituals testified to God's promise not to forsake His inheritance.